A Guide to Becoming a Homeowner for African-Americans (Yes it is different for us)

Quentin Hardy is excellent at his job and has a lot of patience with first time home buyers. He guided my wife and myself every step of the way in purchasing our first home. I would definitely recommend him to anyone that is considering buying a home.
-W. Blalock

"We had a great experience closing on our first home with Quentin. Always there for our 1,000+ questions. We always felt at ease."
T. Gein

"Quentin Hardy and ... Team were amazing. They explained the home buying process to my husband and I. Each step of the way they were there answering our questions. We are so very appreciative of their help. I would use them again and again. I would refer all my friends and family to use the services of Quentin Hardy"
-D. Ramos

"What was undoubtedly a complicated mortgage for me and my wife was made considerably more "normal" thanks to Quentin's patience, dedication and knowledge of our specialized loan. The high level of support and professionalism demonstrated by his team as well can't be overstated. We don't hesitate to refer Quentin Hardy"
-K. Rochefort

EXCELLENT!!!!! Quentin walked me through my mortgage process every step of the way. I laughed, cried and screamed, you name it, I did it, Quentin was right there directing our steps (my husband and I) Fantastic experience. Quentin is a wonderful Mortgage broker but most of all he is a Great and Honest person.
-K. Lodge

"Quentin was so amazing to work with!!! He is very knowledgeable and responded so quickly to any questions we had. He was such a pleasure to work with and we will highly recommend him to any of our friends"
-S. Hanover

Quentin was exceptionally helpful in helping me get my home renovation and mortgage loan. He has been impressively responsive and knowledgeable throughout my entire home buying process. Quentin's delivery on quality and genuine customer service has been and continues to be a constant, and I'm pleased to recommend him.
-J. Tavares

I utilized the services of Quentin Hardy in recent years on my first major home purchase. He was thorough, knowledgeable and above all a consummate professional. As a woman making such a huge financial commitment, it was especially important to me, to feel that the professionals in the process heard me and had my best interest at heart. Quentin Hardy consistently made me feel this way. I will certainly use his services again and would recommend to anyone looking to make real estate transaction(s) to do the same. You will be glad you did. Thanks Quentin!
-M. Freeman

Mr. Hardy is very professional and delivers without a hitch. I've used his services several times and I've recommended him to friends and siblings. All positive reviews!
-C. Ramos

Quentin is professional, knowledgeable, and personable. He helped me get into my first home and I can't thank him enough!
-R. Ruisi

<u>LEGAL NOTICE</u>

About Quentin

Quentin was born in New York City and raised in New York City and nearby Westchester County. Upon graduation from Iona college with honors he moved to Long Island NY. After marrying his long time sweetheart Nena, he lived and worked in Buenos Aires, Argentina for several years and traveled to about a dozen countries expanding his horizons and understanding of the world.

Being born of a Jamaican immigrant mother and an African-American father along with his travels and studies he has developed an atypical perspective on race in America. Along with his wife he has two sons and they live on Long Island NY.

Quentin became a top producer in the mortgage business earning national recognition multiple times throughout his nearly 20 year tenure in the industry. He is also recognized as a national expert in renovation lending.

For fun and exercise he is a practitioner of Brazilian Jiu-jitsu and a fan of MMA.

You can reach Quentin Hardy by calling him directly at 516-697-4200

TABLE OF CONTENTS

PREFACE

Before I write anything else, I want to say thank you for taking the time and picking up my book to read. While reading a book about real estate and mortgage financing isn't the most exciting topic in the world, it is an important one - especially for African-Americans. There is a worsening wealth gap in the United States and Real Estate plays a big role in this.

My goal for the first part of this book is to hopefully engage the reader in understanding that the process of buying and owning a home are indeed different for African-Americans. The goal of this book is to give you a primer so you can become more educated about why you should own, how to navigate the process and then keep the home.

While I would love to help you with your mortgage lending, even if I don't get the opportunity, I hope you get value from my book and find your dream home. If I can help you in any way, please don't hesitate to reach out to me.

Quentin Hardy
516-697-4200

Part One

WHY IS THIS BOOK EVEN NEEDED?

One may ask the above question when reading the title to this book. Isn't buying and owning a home the same for everyone? Currently the Fair Housing Act protects against discrimination of race, color, national origin, religion, sex, familial status, and disability. These laws were initially put in place back in the 1960's. The initial need for these laws and the fact that they are still so relevant today indicates that no, things are not the same for everyone.

Another perspective is that everything is different for us. When medical and pharmaceutical studies are done, frequently there are differences in how black people respond to certain medications. We have different rates of expression of certain diseases. We have different buying patterns and tastes when it comes to food, music and clothing. Our numbers for employment and income are different. We are different from other groups in most things we measure or observe. This does not make us better or worse, just different. Home buying and home ownership are different for us as well.

In Part One of this book we will go into some of the primary differences for African-American homeowners. This is more of the "WHY" part of the book. Part Two is more about "HOW" and the steps to take when becoming a homeowner.

Chapter 1 - The Wealth Gap

Household wealth is simply the household's assets minus its debt. It is important that we distinguish the difference between wealth and income. Income will not make you wealthy. What you do with your income will determine if you become wealthy or not. While we hear talk of income inequality, wealth inequality is an even more dire situation for us. The average White household is worth 86 times more than its Black counterpart[1].

If you would like a brief video explanation check out the link to a video done by Attorney and Emmy Nominated Film Producer Antonio Moore that is about one minute long
https://youtu.be/2hGz6r2PndE

In the United States today there is a tremendous gap between the wealth of Aftican-Americans and the wealth of other groups. The greatest challenge with this disparity is that we did not come by this honestly. In his 1964 book, *Why We Can't Wait*, Martin Luther King, Jr. wrote, "It is obvious that if a man is entered at the starting line of a race three hundred years after another man, the first would have to perform some impossible feat in order to catch up with his fellow runner." MLK the master dreamer used the word "impossible" in this instance. Basically African-Americans were not allowed to participate in many wealth building endeavors in this county for hundreds of years. This means the other groups

---

[1] "The Racial Wealth Gap: Addressing America's Most Pressing ...." 18 Feb. 2018, https://www.forbes.com/sites/brianthompson1/2018/02/18/the-racial-wealth-gap-addressing-americas-most-pressing-epidemic/. Accessed 18 Jan. 2020.

that did participate had several hundreds of years to build wealth and then pass that wealth to their descendants.

According to Demos.Org in 2011 the median white household had $111,146 in wealth holdings, compared to just $7,113 for the median Black household. That 300 year head start is partially responsible for this. Black people in the United States own about 2.6% of the nation's wealth. The challenge however is that this percentage is shrinking. The Institute for Policy Studies report The Road to Zero Wealth: How the Racial Divide is Hollowing Out the America's Middle Class showed that between 1983 and 2013, the wealth of the median black household declined 75 percent (from $6,800 to $1,700) while over the same period of time, wealth for the median white household increased 14 percent from $102,000 to $116,800. If this trend continues the median black household will have a net worth of $0.00 by 2053. That's right ZERO NET WORTH. This is economic extinction.

Now I know you picked up a book about becoming a homeowner and I'm hitting you with facts and figures about the Black Wealth Gap and discussing Economic Extinction. That's some heavy stuff. My brother was a G.I. Joe fan and everytime I see him he finds a way to interject his favorite phrase into the conversation "knowing is half the battle". In this case it is appropriate.

We need to act and act now. You need to act and act now. I don't want to sound like Chicken Little but the sky is falling.

There is good news however. While there is no simple fix or quick solution it turns out that "Eliminating disparities in homeownership rates and returns would substantially reduce the racial wealth gap.[2] We will talk more about homeownership rates and returns in later chapters. For now understand that if you are not a homeowner yet, becoming one can help increase your household net worth and begin or improve the generational wealth situation for your family. If you are already a homeowner, please encourage your friends and family to also become homeowners. If you are in a position to do so, you may also want to consider buying another home as an investment property to further take advantage of the impact real estate can have on your worth.

If I were to tell you that the average homeowner has a greater net worth than the average renter you would not likely be surprised. Let me ask you, how many times greater is the average net worth of a homeowner in comparison to the average net worth of a renter? Could it be 5 times as much? Maybe 10 times? Would you believe that the average net worth of a homeowner is 44 times greater than that of a renter?![3] So for many families the single greatest thing they can do to improve their financial position, the single greatest thing they can do to increase net worth, the single greatest thing they can do to make progress in generating generational wealth is to own (and keep) a home.

---

[2] "The Racial Wealth Gap: Why Policy Matters | Demos." https://www.demos.org/research/racial-wealth-gap-why-policy-matters. Accessed 11 Jan. 2020.
[3] "The Net Worth of a Homeowner is 44x Greater Than A Renter ...." 20 Aug. 2018, https://www.keepingcurrentmatters.com/en/2018/08/20/the-net-worth-of-a-homeowner-is-44x-greater-than-a-renter/. Accessed 11 Jan. 2020.

Chapter 2 - Homeownership Rates

In the 1960's The Fair Housing Act gave Black families new access to homeownership. The rate of homeownership increased for years after that. In the last few years however the homeownership rates have declined. In fact it has declined to the point where black homeownership rates today are about the same as they were when discriminitation was legal.[4]

Basically all gains in Black Home Ownership since the Fair Housing Act was passed have been erased since the year 2000.

The history of homeownership by generation is particularly troubling. This view shows that the prospects for black homeownership have gone from hopeful to pessimistic in only 15 years.

"About half of black people born in the last 10 years of the baby boom (1956–65) were homeowners by the time they turned 50. The early gen Xers (born 1966–75) had a higher homeownership rate in 2000 (when they were in their late 20s and early 30s) than the late boomers had enjoyed 10 years earlier. But the financial and housing crisis slowed early gen Xers' transition into homeownership from 2000 to 2010 (when they were in their 30s and early 40s) and caused more of this generation to lose their homes than to become owners after 2010. This retrocession is unprecedented for any other generation or age group.

---

[4] "African American Homeownership Falls to 50-year Low ...." http://www.nareb.com/african-american-homeownership-falls-50-year-low/. Accessed 11 Jan. 2020.

The picture only gets worse for younger black generations. Those born from 1976 to 1985—spanning late gen Xers and early millennials—have barely begun their homeownership transition, but they're getting an even slower start than either of the two older cohorts."[5]

The decline in homeownership among African-American can be attributed to many factors including a higher rate of foreclosure (another whole topic for another chapter), predatory lending by banks, increasing income disparity between races and even cultural differences.

Now you the reader can not fix this for everyone but you can certainly change your situation and at the same time impact the probability of your descendants. Children raised in homes their parents owned, rather than rented, were nearly three-times as likely to buy a home themselves.[6]

---

[5] "Are gains in black homeownership history? | Urban Institute." 14 Feb. 2017, https://www.urban.org/urban-wire/are-gains-black-homeownership-history. Accessed 11 Jan. 2020.

[6] "Family Tradition: Kids Are More Likely to Own a Home If Their ...." 10 Aug. 2016, https://www.trulia.com/research/family-tradition/. Accessed 11 Jan. 2020.

Chapter 3 - Red Lining & Discrimination

Housing

In the 1960s the sociologist John McKnight coined this term. It was used to describe the discriminatory practice of drawing a red line on the map where banks would avoid investments based on community demographics.

The National Housing Act of 1934 was passed as part of the"New Deal" orchestrated by President Franklin D. Roosevelt. This introduced concepts like the 30 year mortgage and fixed interest rates. Suddenly a group of people who could not previously buy a home suddenly had a new opportunity. This was all new to all involved. They had to come up with a way to measure the risk of the loans to ensure repayment. One of the things they did was draw maps and assign risk to different neighborhoods. The lowest risk or best neighborhood was green. That was for business people. Blue was second best and for white collar workers. Yellow was a declining area with those from the working class. Red was considered hazardous. Those were neighborhoods with poor whites, foreign born residents and "Negros" (the word used at the time this was authored). Although people in the Red areas were not more likely to default on their mortgages they were still not granted the same access to loans.

The impact of Redlining is still apparent in the United States. If you can tolerate the profanity in the opening clip from comedian

Chris Rock you can watch this NPR video for a more in depth explanation, otherwise skip the first 12 seconds
https://youtu.be/O5FBJyqfoLM

   Although the practice of Redlining is illegal it still is happening today. The Brookings Institute found Homes of similar quality in neighborhoods with similar amenities are worth 23 percent less ($48,000 per home on average, amounting to $156 billion in cumulative losses) in majority black neighborhoods, compared to those with very few or no black residents.[7] IF you prefer a short video on the current state of Redlining MSNBC did an 8 minute video on the topic
https://www.msnbc.com/b810fdb0-acf1-4ec6-868e-225b2d54ca6a

   Now I would make the case that you are still better off being a homeowner in a red lined neighborhood in most situations rather than being a renter elsewhere. Of course being able to avoid being redlined is the most favorable position.

   Where I live in New York is one of the top 10 most segregated areas in the country. A newspaper recently did a multi-year investigation into the discriminatory practices that keep this area so segregated. Although this is happening in the area of the country where I live, do not think this is unique. It is happening across the country in varying degrees. The journalists had teams of testers record audio and video of interactions with real estate agents. It turns out that about half of the interactions resulted in redlining or other discriminatory practices by the real

___

[7] "The devaluation of assets in black neighborhoods - Brookings ...." 27 Nov. 2018, https://www.brookings.edu/research/devaluation-of-assets-in-black-neighborhoods/. Accessed 11 Jan. 2020.

estate agents[8]. The documentary is over 40 minutes long and worth viewing. The URL is in the citation at the bottom of this page. Of course the toughest part of this is that you don't know when you are being redlined or discriminated against. Until you have the experience of another person or group, you can not compare to yours. Using pairs of testers allowed us to see how the same story garners a different reaction if one is Black or not.

So how do you keep from being a victim of redlining? Well if you Google how to avoid redlining when buying a home or buying real estate you are likely to see many articles and videos about redlining but few if any at all about how to avoid redlining. The reality is that you must do this yourself. If your real estate professional is helping pick neighborhoods be sure to understand the criteria they are using. Are they putting you in a certain neighborhood because it is populated by a majority of people who look like you or did they pick it based on criteria you requested? Now you may still buy in a predominantly Black neighborhood. Just be sure it is your choice and not someone deciding where you should live. Be aware. Also know that your budget may very well be the biggest determining factor. Where can you afford to buy? Again I would say you are better off buying and owning where you can afford rather than renting elsewhere.

Lending

Redlining and discrimination impact housing and neighborhood selection and of course it is also a factor in the arena of lending. I have seen this first hand. At one time I worked at one

[8] "Long Island Divided: Testing the Divide - Newsday." https://projects.newsday.com/long-island/real-estate-investigation-videos/. Accessed 11 Jan. 2020.

of the nation's top lending institutions. I also lived in a predominantly Black neighborhood. I heard a representative from the bank where I worked was coming to speak at my local PTA. I could throw a baseball from my backyard and hit the school it was so close to my home. My wife and I were members of the PTA. We were involved in the school. Who better to represent the bank than me right? Nope. Another loan officer was chosen. He was from my office but not my neighborhood. I asked to have it switched since I was a more logical choice. They explained that it would not be switched. The loan officer who was selected to cover that area was the subprime Loan Officer who would offer higher rates and less favorable terms on these subprime loans. Why would the bank push these less favorable, higher fee, higher interest rate, poorer terms loans on a specific community? Should each person receive the best loan for which they qualify? It was never explained why the subprime loan officer would be the choice. I did not originate subprime loans. Were the subprime loan officers targeting minority neighborhoods? In 2006, at the height of the boom, Black and Hispanic families making more than $200,000 a year were more likely on average to be given a subprime loan than a white family making less than $30,000 a year.[9] Plain and simple: yes.

Now of course that was years ago and this could no longer happen right? It is illegal now. Well it was illegal then and it still happened. To this day I see people in the mortgage business give loans to people based on what is best for the bank or the commission for the loan officer and not what is best for the consumer. As a matter of fact some lenders target these people and

---

[9] "The Dramatic Racial Bias of Subprime Lending During the ...." 16 Aug. 2013, https://www.citylab.com/equity/2013/08/blacks-really-were-targeted-bogus-loans-during-housing-boom/6559/. Accessed 11 Jan. 2020.

neighborhoods. It is a historical irony. The neighborhoods and people they once avoided are now their targets in a form of reverse-redlining.

African-Americans can be from 250% as likely to be denied a mortgage to 20% more likely depending upon which statistics and which method one uses to measure this. The problematic reality however is that regardless of methodology the result is the same: when we control for all variables it seems you are more likely to be denied a loan just because you are Black. A yearlong analysis of over 31 million records indicates that modern-day redlining exists in lending today[10]

So how can you avoid these discriminatory practices and situations when you go to get a mortgage? Be aware. Again the answer is that it is up to you. Ask questions. Why am I getting this kind of loan? How did you come to this recommendation for me? Your loan officer or home mortgage consultant or whatever he or she is called, should be able to explain what loan programs were considered and why they are recommending what they are recommending. It is up to you to protect yourself.

---

[10] "Modern-day redlining: How banks block people of color from ...." 15 Feb. 2018, https://www.chicagotribune.com/business/ct-biz-modern-day-redlining-201802 15-story.html. Accessed 11 Jan. 2020.

Chapter 4 - Foreclosure

Let's talk about the "F" word: Foreclosure. Foreclosure is a legal process in which a lender attempts to recover the balance of a loan from a borrower who has stopped making payments to the lender by forcing the sale of the home. Simply put, someone stops paying the mortgage and the bank takes the home and sells it. The prior owner loses any equity and usually ruins their credit for years to come.

African-Americans have a higher rate of foreclosure than do other groups. It is estimated that Black homeowners are nearly 1.75 times more likely to experience foreclosure than their White counterparts[11]. This happens even if we move into a predominantly white neighborhood so it is not a redlining kind of thing.[12] In the words of Treach from Naught by Nature "No matter where you go, there you are".

If this is the case it would be smart to learn how to avoid foreclosure even before buying the home in the first place. So let's discuss how.

First when the bank approves you for a loan, they are using your debt to income ratio. They are looking at your gross income and comparing it to your current financial obligations and determining how much space (capacity) you have for more

---

[11] "NEW RESEARCH "Foreclosures by Race and Ethnicity: The ...." https://www.responsiblelending.org/mortgage-lending/research-analysis/foreclosures-by-race-presentation.pdf. Accessed 11 Jan. 2020.

[12] "Higher rates of foreclosure follow black ... - Phys.org." 7 Feb. 2019, https://phys.org/news/2019-02-higher-foreclosure-black-homeowners-white.html. Accessed 11 Jan. 2020.

payments. They are not factoring in whether or not you are saving for a child's education or sending them to private school already, they do not look at how much that vacation is going to cost, they don't know if your son or daughter is taking Brazilian Jiu-Jitsu classes (highly recommended by the way for the whole family!) or dance. The bank doesn't know your real budget. The bigger question: do you? This is step one. Prepare a budget and know what you can afford. I do believe in stretching if need be to get into the home but this may require you to cut some other things. When my wife and I bought our first home we did not have cable tv. Cable is not a utility. We didn't take any expensive vacations and neither of us had any hobbies with cost associated with it. I didn't go to the gym. I became a runner because running shoes are a manageable expense. We went to our local public library and borrowed VHS tapes of the Sopranos or movies. We didn't even go to Blockbuster (yes this was years ago) to rent movies. I would go to my parents' home and record Sesame Street episodes so my children had something to watch. We even bought a home with a second unit so there was an income to help us pay the mortgage. Keep in mind this was not permanent. After 5 years we sold that home and used the proceeds to move to a nicer home in a nicer area. So the point is to buy a home you can afford.

Second is to be prepared for "Murphy". You've heard of Murphy's Law right? Anything that can go wrong will go wrong. Now it might not be that gloomy but things will go wrong. Do you have proper homeowners insurance coverage, life insurance and health insurance? Speak with your financial planner or appropriate professional to be sure you are protected.

Now this is all the same for everybody. What is the main difference in the foreclosure rate for Black families?

We already discussed one when we mentioned discrimination in lending. Getting a more expensive loan than necessary. The subprime scandal hit our community harder than others. The fact that unemployment is about double in African-American vs Whites is another factor.

We are more leveraged than our White counterparts. "The average first home purchased by black homebuyers is valued at $127,000, compared with $139,000 for white homebuyers, yet black homebuyers, on average, have higher mortgage debt ($90,000) than white homebuyers ($75,000). Surprisingly and notably, the difference in mortgage debt ($15,000) is larger than the difference in the home value ($12,000)."[13] Some of this is again due to the gap discussed in chapter one. This is anecdotal but when I see a white family buying their first home and getting a gift from family it is not uncommon for the gift to be $40,000, $50,000 or sometimes over $100,000 (I live in the expensive suburbs of New York City). If they are short on funds they frequently can call grandma and get a few thousand. On the other hand when I see Black families getting a gift from family it is rarely over $10,000 and sometimes under $5,000.

So here is the solution "Money can protect yourself from almost anything, but Black families tend not to have access to accumulated or inherited wealth,"[14]

---

[13] "Higher rates of foreclosure follow black ... - Phys.org." 7 Feb. 2019, https://phys.org/news/2019-02-higher-foreclosure-black-homeowners-white.html. Accessed 11 Jan. 2020.

[14] "Higher rates of foreclosure follow black ... - Phys.org." 7 Feb. 2019, https://phys.org/news/2019-02-higher-foreclosure-black-homeowners-white.html. Accessed 11 Jan. 2020.

Here is how it works: a family falls behind on payments so they call their other family members for help. That's great when your family has the resources to help. This again is more about wealth than income. If your family has little or no wealth, no one can help you long enough to even buy the time to sell the home so you fall behind and never catch up. The members of our society with the lowest median wealth (yeah that's us) would then be the most likely to not have someone to help.

The solution? Reserves. What are reserves? Funds or material set aside or saved for future use. If you are a Dave Ramsey fan you would call this an Emergency Fund. Set aside money knowing that Murphy will visit and bring his law with him. A storm is coming, we just don't know when. If you have money in your reserves you can weather the storm and come out dry rather than losing your shirt (and your home). Don't expect your family will be able to help. Put aside you reserves as soon as you get into the home. Keep saving so you can protect your home.

Recently a family friend was recounting the story of a foreclosure which happened in her family. Her family member was a TSA agent making a six figure income. She looked good, smelled good, always had her hair and nails done. She had inherited a home from family. When there was a government shutdown she missed a couple of paychecks, fell behind on the mortgage and never recovered. Don't do that. If you can't weather the storm of one or two missed paychecks, when Murphy shows up and he will, you are doomed.

Chapter 5 - Bottom Line

The bottom line is that the homeownership process is different for us. Keeping that home is different for us. Securing a loan is different for us. Rather than ignoring those differences and allowing them to harm or hurt you I propose you be aware and prepared for the impact of those differences.

We need higher rates of homeownership in our community to help aid in our overall economic well being. Becoming a homeowner helps you, your children, your family and creates an example for others in our community. Owning your own home (or real estate) is one of the pillars of generational wealth.

Chapter 6 - My Personal Real Estate Journey

When my wife and I moved back to New York she was pregnant with our first child. Our plan was to stay a few months with my parents while I got a new job, saved money for a home and then we would buy. The task was taking longer than expected and we were having trouble qualifying for a loan partially due to my prior overseas employment and 4 year absence from the United States.

My wife and I discussed this and decided we should just rent for the time being and "things will get better". My parents explained things don't "get better" one must make them better. They were adamant about us not renting. Their idea was that once we started renting it would become increasingly difficult to save money while at the same time housing prices would increase and maybe even increase at a rate faster than we could save.

We decided to take their advice. We had both lived in homes owned by our parents while being raised, so renting was foreign to us and less comfortable than owning. Both my wife and I also value our parent's wisdom and guidance. We are fortunate to have them in our lives as positive influencers.

Eventually we found a home with a second income (a two-family home with rental income) that we could make work. My wife's father had to co-sign for us and even help with the down payment. Decades later I still thank him as now I understand the impact these moves made on our overall economic trajectory and current wealth.

We bought a two-family home for $160,000 (that included a seller's concession to cover closing costs as part of the mortgage) in 1998 and sold it for $316,500 in 2003. We just about doubled our money in 5 years. What else could I have done to increase my familial net worth that much in that period of time? Keep in mind that it costs no working hours or time investment. The funds "invested" would have gone to rent otherwise and been gone. This was money I was going to spend anyway and I used it to increase my wealth.

When we sold it we used the increase to buy a bigger nicer home in a better area. Later we pulled some equity out of that home to buy an investment property. The next step was an even nicer home with superior amenities and space. Now we are looking for another investment property. All of this is a cascade that was caused by that first home. If we had not bought that first home we would not be where we are now.

I hope you will one day get to write your story and that your story is even better than mine. I do know that it only happens if you buy that first one. So let's get to it...

Part Two

Chapter 1 - Overview

If you are currently living in an apartment or renting a house, you may be thinking about buying a home of your own for yourself and your family. This can be an exciting time. Looking at properties, deciding whether to buy a home or build a new one, and finding financing will take up a lot of your time.

There will be a long list of things you will need to do before you buy a home. This list includes:

- Finding the right neighborhood
- Finding a home that is big enough
- Finding the features you are looking for
- Choosing the right size yard
- Choosing a real estate agent
- Understanding the housing market
- The ins and outs of home inspection
- Arranging Financing (get your pre-approval letter)
- Making an offer, and
- Reading contracts

This list does not include all of the decorating, home improvement, and other decisions you will have to make once you have purchased the home.

If you are a first time home buyer, you may be nervous about finding the right home, investing money on a down payment, and being approved for financing. Once you have found a home, it will usually take between two or three months before you will be able to move in. In the meantime, you should plan the following:

- Moving arrangements
- Home inspections
- Yard sales
- Budgeting for paint and other supplies
- Taking time off from work
- Finding a lawyer

Proper planning will help you transition into your new home much easier than if you wait until the last minute to deal with these details. If you are planning on moving yourself, you should find a few friends or family members that will be willing to help as soon as possible.

New Homes vs. Older Homes

Another decision you will have to make is whether to buy a new home or look for an older one. Most first time home buyers usually buy an older home, but this should not deter you from visiting a few builders to see what they are charging for the size of the home you are looking for.

Older homes may cost less, but they can be riddled with problems. In this book, you will learn what to look for when viewing a home, what to include in your purchase offer, and what to expect from a home inspection. There are many older homes that will need only minor repairs. You may even want to consider buying a home in need of repairs and include repairs or renovation as part of your mortgage loan.

Which Home to Choose?

After you have looked into all of your options, you will be wondering which home to choose. There are many ways to find the home that is right for you. When looking at homes, you should keep these criteria in mind:

- Size
- Price
- Neighborhood
- Mortgage payments
- Repairs, and
- Additional features

While this is a short list, throughout this book you will learn other ways to find your dream home. In the end you will just know when you have found the right home.

Moving into your first home will be an experience you will never forget. You should be excited as this is a little piece of the world that is just yours. Whether this is the home in which you will you will live for a long time or just for a short time, buying a home will give you a sense of pride and purpose. Not only will you have a mortgage to pay, you will also be responsible for making the home your own. When thinking about purchasing as home, you should begin saving your money for closing costs, repairs, and decorating materials.

One of the more rewarding moments will be when you get the keys to your new home and you begin making it your own with a little paint, furniture, and personal style.

Chapter 2 - Location, Location, Location

Choosing where to live is almost as important as the type of home you want to live in. While this is a very personal decision, there are pros and cons to every neighborhood. But wherever you want to live, you will have to know where the highways are located, grocery stores, schools, and how far from work you will be. Buying a home means more than the structure you will be living in. It is also the community and the accessibility to places and events that mean the most to you and your family.

Finding the Right Neighborhood

How will you know you have found the right neighborhood? There are many ways to tell:

- You may feel a sense of calm
- The neighborhood may remind you of a happy memory
- You will be close to places you frequent often
- The neighborhood aesthetics are pleasing, or
- The rest of your family is pleased

You may feel one emotion or five when you turn the corner onto the street where you want to live. This will be an exciting time, especially if you have been searching for a home for the past few months.

When looking for the right location, you should consider the following:

- How clean is this neighborhood?
- Is this a high crime area?
- What is the average home value in the neighborhood?
- Are there community bylaws?
- What is the home close to?
- What are the schools like?
- Not glamorous but can you afford it?

While these questions may not include everything you are looking for when buying a home, they should be considered carefully as they will affect your life once you move into the home.

How Clean is this Neighborhood?

You should look at the neighborhood at different times during the day to see how those who live in the neighborhood take care of it. If there is a lot of trash on the ground, the yards are not kept up properly, or there are old signs posted on trees and telephone poles, then the neighborhood may not be for you.

If the neighborhood looks clean and you see people outside caring for their lawns, then you may have found a community of people who care about where they live. This is an important factor if you are planning on living in the neighborhood for many years. All too often people will buy homes only to discover that they live in a neighborhood where people do not have respect for their property or the property of others. This can make selling the home much more difficult in the future.

Is this a High Crime Area?

While all neighborhoods will experience some crime, you should consider buying a home in an area that has a high crime rate very carefully. While the home itself may be the right price for your budget, it may not be located in an area that is right for your well-being.

Drive by the neighborhood at nighttime to see if there is adequate street lighting, suspicious activity, or anything else that might cause you to use caution. Research the neighborhood and find out how the crime rate compares with other neighborhoods. If the crime rate is too high, then it may be best to look somewhere else.

You are likely better off with less home in a safer neighborhood rather than buying a more spacious or nicer home in a high crime area. Your safety is even more important than your comfort.

What is the Average Home Value in the Neighborhood?

You can find this information out very easily by asking your real estate agent or by looking up this information at the county clerk's office or on their website. You should be aware of the home values that are in your neighborhood for several reasons:

- Housing prices will vary depending on the neighborhood and region. You want to buy a home that you will be able to make a profit when you decide to sell.
- You do not want to pay too much for a home.
- Giving a solid offer for the home means knowing what other homes that are similar in size are selling for.

Are there Community Bylaws or HOAs?

If you are looking at a home that is inside a community or homeowners association (HOA = HomeOwner Association), you should be aware of yearly dues, rules about what can be in your yard (pool, lawn decorations, etc.) and any other rules that they may have.

Many people enjoy living in an HOA community because they feel safe and want to meet others in the neighborhood. HOAs usually have picnics and other events during the year where neighbors can meet each other. Some communities have pools, tennis courts, and other amenities. Traditionally, you will find these to be townhouses or condominiums.

What is the Home Close to?

When choosing a home, you will need to find the nearest grocery stores, schools, route to work, and other necessities that will make living in the neighborhood more convenient. Drive around the neighborhood to see what is around it. This will help make your decision to buy a home in a particular neighborhood much easier.

When my wife and I were looking to buy our first home we had a unique experience with a proximity situation. As we toured the home I saw people walk through the back yard, lift up a portion of the fence and go through to the other block behind us. It turned out that this home's yard was uniquely positioned to allow a shortcut to another block due to a dead end and no way to walk around. We found out that not only would all the students attending the school cut through this yard every morning and every afternoon going to and from school, but it was also a good short cut for the local gang members to use to quickly get from point a to point b.

Year later when looking to purchase the home we live in now, the realtor gave us directions to the home. The directions seemed a little indirect to me. We drove from that house in what I thought was the more direct route. It was more direct but also took us through a part of town we would not want to be near.

In both cases the homes were desirable but the location was not. Check out the surrounding area.

What are the schools like?

While you may or may not have children, this is still a consideration. The quality of the schools and their overall performance attract or deter families from buying in an area. If you are not a parent and don't plan on becoming one, you should still be aware of the school districts and their impact on the value of the home and the ability to sell a home in the future.

Of course if you are a parent the school district will have different value to you. The academic performance of the school should be considered along with other factors you find important to you. Is the size of the school population important? Are the extra curricular activities important? Do they offer any special programs you or your child may find of interest or necessary?

Some parents may be concerned about the diversity of the school. Realize there is only so much your real estate agent can answer or discuss about certain topics and this is one where they may not be able to share much information. If this is a consideration for you visit the school or look it up online. With the internet today one can either find out this information or look at photos of events at the school to see who is attending the school

Is there Garbage Pickup?

While this may not seem like something you are interested in, when it comes to disposing of your trash, you may need to haul it to the dump yourself. Ask about trash pickup so that you can decide if this is something you really want to do on the weekend. This really is a question of living within the city limits or living in the country.

Living near the city or far from the city or in the city

Choosing the neighborhood you want to live in will also include deciding whether you want to live in a city, near a city in the suburbs or in the country. Many people with families want to live in the suburbs because there is more room for children to grow, but is still close enough for parents to commute to work in the city. Some choose the country so they have more space and fewer people around. Others of course prefer city living and the idea of a variety of people and things to do.

But there are advantages to living closer or further from the city as well. Those who live near the city may be closer to work, restaurants, activities, and events. Those who live further from the city's border may have a longer commute to work, but they will be able to enjoy the peace and quiet of having fewer people around them. Of course if you live and work in the suburbs or the country this changes your options, especially when it comes to commuting.

In many cases the proximity to the city will have an impact on the value of the home. Having easy access to public transportation is another consideration. For city commuters, being within walking distance of the this type of transportation has value. Being near them, even if you don't use them, can impact the value of the home.

About 75% of Black households live in metropolitan areas[15]. This likely means many of the readers will have grown up in or reside in a metropolitan area. Don't be afraid to break from this. It may be out of your comfort zone. Just be aware of this when making a decision, so it is not overly emotional or too heavily biased towards staying where you are used to being.

Whichever lifestyle you prefer, you should construct a pros and cons list that will give you a better idea of what to expect

---

[15] "Why Do Blacks Live in The Cities and Whites Live in the ...." http://www-siepr.stanford.edu/workp/swp00007.pdf. Accessed 18 Jan. 2020.

when looking for a home. Once you have looked at your list, you will have a better idea of which to choose.

You should check out what is it like to live closer or further away from the city. While there will always be pros and cons, you should be able to find a home that will help you lead the type of lifestyle that is important to you and your family.

Making the Commute

You will have to count on the amount of traveling you will have to endure to and from your job when buying your first home. Unless you are relocating, you will have to find a neighborhood that is close enough to drive to or is accessible by public transportation. While some people enjoy sitting on a bus or train for an hour during the day, you may not want to use your time this way. Unfortunately, living in the suburbs may require you to make a longer commute. Living in the city may mean your trip to work is only a few minutes. In some cities one doesn't need a car or a family may get by with one. Consider this in your overall finance picture and budget.

If you want to remain relatively close to your job, you should establish a distance threshold. Inform your real estate agent of your geographic limit or travel time limit. Also realize some neighborhoods are easier to drive in and out than others. It is not only the distance but the road system that takes you to and from the places you are going. My parents live only a few minutes from my home but there is only one main road to get there. When there is traffic or rain the delay is dramatic. The people commuting from there have a tough time anytime it snows or rains hard during their commute. You should find different roads as well as highway accessible roads that will make your commute easier.

If you take some type of public transportation you must figure that into your mental equation. Sometimes people commuting to the city will travel a little further if the train or bus will be their primary commuting vehicle. Not having to drive or having the ability to read or check e-mail or nap can change the complexion of one's commute.

You should also look for a home during different times of day in order to figure out the traffic patterns. If possible, live in an area that goes against normal traffic patterns. That way you will not be stuck in traffic going to work or when coming home. For those commuting to the city see if you can commute earlier or later than standard rush hours and will that make a difference.

Commuting to work can easily be over an hour for many working in major metro areas. While this may be inevitable, you should consider all of your options before purchasing a home.

Schools in the Area

If you have school age children, then you will want to find a home that is close to schools in the area. This goes for both public and private schools. If you find a neighborhood that you like, find out which school district it is located in. Not all school districts are alike and you will have to send your children to the school district your home is located in. Don't assume that the school districts line up with the neighborhood lines either. Sometimes part of a town may have a different school district than another part. I've seen identical homes across the street from each other have values that are ten of thousands of dollars different simply because of the school district.

While your children do not have to walk to school, being relatively close to home will make it easier to pick them up, participate in after school events, and give them a sense of community.

Be sure to weigh all of your options when choosing a home if you have children. Also, find out where the middle school and high schools are in the area. Eventually, your children will be attending these schools. Be prepared and find out everything you can about these schools as well.

Grocery Shopping and Other Necessities

Before buying a home, survey the area to see what is available. This will give you a good idea of what it would be like to live in the area. Spend a few days there if possible. This will save you from making a huge mistake later on.

While living in the country or the suburbs may seem peaceful, be prepared to do a lot more driving. The nearest grocery store or pharmacy may be thirty minutes or more. This is another factor you will have to consider when buying your first home. While small towns have centralized areas where the shops and grocery stores are located, unless you live in town, you will have to drive in order to get there. This is less of an issue than it was years ago as more and more services and shopping are done online and things just show up at your door.

If you are planning to stay in the city, you will have the advantages of public transportation, but you may still need a car for larger grocery shops. While the city can be convenient in many ways, parking a car is not one of them. You will have to pay for garage parking in many instances, which will end up costing you more money than if you lived in the country or the suburbs. You will be able to get to these stores quickly and easily at any time during the day.

What other stores or services do you need nearby? Do you frequent an organic produce store? Do you take group exercise classes? Do you practice a martial art? Do you want to live near a gym with a squash court? Different people have different desires. These things have an impact on your quality of life

Other Location Considerations

Other location considerations include:
- Weather
- Road conditions
- Location of property in the neighborhood, and
- Room to grow
- Flood Zones

You should be thinking ahead in terms of the weather. If you are planning on living in the country, for example, you should pay attention to possible flooding, snow, and other weather that could affect you getting to work. If the road is a dirt road, you should ask if the county will clear the road and how often they will do so. This is another advantage of living in the city because you could always use public transportation if you do not want to drive. In certain areas your choice of vehicle is impacted as well. Will you need a different vehicle to get around during inclement weather in the neighborhood you like?

The location of the property is also important. If the property is located at the bottom of a slope, you may have flooding issues after a rainstorm. Also, as your family grows, you many need more room. You should find property that can hold a home addition if necessary if this may be a consideration in your future. Investigating in a home requires a great deal of thought and planning. Even if you do not have a family, you should find a home that will allow you to grow as your interests change.

White Flight

This may or may not be a concern for all buyers. White Flight is when a neighborhood reaches a certain threshold of Non-Whites and the Whites move out of that neighborhood. In the suburbs, a lot of white residents still prefer living around other whites—and they're willing to uproot their families to make that happen.[16] If you want to live in an African-American or mostly minority neighborhood this may not be a concern. When looking for a diverse neighborhood this may be a consideration. The issue becomes when a group wants so much to not live in a neighborhood that they begin dropping the prices of their home in order to get out. If you see a neighborhood where this has been happening and you are ok with living there, you may find some motivated sellers. You may not like their motivation but a deal is a deal. If you find a neighborhood which is just starting to have this

---

[16] "'White Flight' Remains a Reality - Pacific Standard." 6 Mar. 2018, https://psmag.com/social-justice/white-flight-remains-a-reality. Accessed 18 Jan. 2020.

happen be aware values may not rise (or even drop) until the neighborhood has been "reset" with the new population.

Chapter 3 - Working With Realtors

If you are like many people, chances are good you looked around different neighborhoods, saw a few homes that were for sale, maybe visited an open house or two, and then felt stuck. What is the next step? Approach the homeowner? Visit the real estate agent?

Finding the right real estate agent when buying a home depends on what you are looking for in a home. You may have to visit several real estate agents before finding one that listens to your wants and needs. After all, you should be comfortable working with them during the house hunting process.

Choosing a Realtor

There are a few ways to find a reliable real estate agent. For example, you can:

- Ask friends and family
- Ask other real estate agents
- Attend a few open houses and meet real estate agents
- Find ads online or in the newspaper
- Walk into a local office, or
- Look for local real estate agents in your neighborhood by paying attention to for sale signs in the neighborhood

- If you are local to me, ask me for my list of personally endorsed agents – these are agents that I have interviewed, screened, and meet my high standards and my personal seal of endorsement!

Asking plenty of questions before looking at houses may seem like a lot of work, but when you visit a real estate agent for the first time, you should think about questions that will help you get to know this person who is going to help you find your dream home. Here are a few good questions to ask:

1. Are you a certified real estate agent? (While all agents need to be licensed in all the states they are selling properties in, not all real estate agents belong to the National Association of Realtors. Have a conversation with your real estate agent about the pros and cons of each which vary by geography)
2. How long have you been in the real estate business?
3. Which neighborhoods are you most familiar with?
4. How many homes do you have that will fit my needs?
5. What is your typical commission on a home in my price range?

Once you have asked these questions, you should be looking for honest and complete answers, good communication, and eye contact. These are the questions that the real estate agent should have practice in answering and should not have to give you a standard 'salesperson' answer. Also pay close attention to the questions they ask you.

If you feel uncomfortable, then you are under no obligation to continue with this real estate agent even if they have some good property matches to show you. Normally, if a real estate agent does not have properties that fit what you are looking for, they will recommend you to another real estate agent in the group. This is also a good sign because it shows that the group is looking out for your interests and the interest of its employees.

You should also pay attention to:

- How well your real estate agent listens to what you are looking for
- How well they understand current real estate law
- How many other clients they seem to have
- How they speak to their coworkers
- How often they communicate with you on the phone or by email
- Online reviews or absence of these reviews

In the end, you will have to be the judge of the real estate agent. If they know what you are talking about, can find out information you need quickly, and are willing to take time to listen to what you need, then you should work very well with them.

In some cases, you may be asked to sign an agreement that states you will only be working with a specific real estate agency or agent when looking for a home. You are under no obligation to sign this paperwork and you should only do so if you feel very comfortable.

While these agreements are not binding, it could make a difference in your home buying down the road. Only sign agreements if you feel very comfortable.

During your search for a real estate agent, you will find a variety of agents that will want to work with you. These include:

- Experienced agents
- New agents
- Pushy agents
- Absentee agents, and
- Hard working agents

While all real estate agents have different personalities, you will have to decide which one you will want to work with when looking for your new home.

Experienced Agents vs. New Agents

This is an age old debate that should be addressed. While an experienced agent may have sold more homes and earned more commissions, new agents can be just as helpful and need to get some sales under their belt, which may prompt them to work harder for you.

While you should ask about their experience, you should take into consideration other traits such as the ability to listen and the ability to show you homes in your price range. Experienced agents and new agents have been trained in similar fashion and only have their personalities to bring to the table.

There are experienced agents out there who will drag their feet because they are over confident or they are not as interested in their jobs as they once were. Experienced agents may know more about different neighborhoods, but some of them are not as proactive as they used to be.

You should not let inexperience deter you when looking for an agent. Many times new agents will work harder because they want to gain a reputation that they can use to build confidence in their future clients.

Pushy Agents

Unfortunately, you will meet real estate agents who will want to sell you more than you need. In an effort to earn larger commissions or sell those properties that are more difficult, many agents will try this tactic. This is where you will need to stand firm. You do not want to waste your time looking at homes that are beyond your price range unless you can find a way to lower the price.

While looking at possible homes is exciting, this will not last long as you will grow weary of spending all of your available time looking for a home. If an agent keeps showing you homes that are out of your price range, then you should consider finding another agent.

Absentee Agents

Absentee real estate agents are those agents who show you a few homes and then disappear for a few weeks. These agents may be overworked, may not be able to find a home in your price range or neighborhood, or have higher priced commissions to find. Whatever the reasons, this is unprofessional behavior and should be rectified immediately, especially if you need to find a home quickly.

If an agent does not have homes in your price range or neighborhood, they should recommend another agent in the group. Agencies never want to lose customers. If your agent does not do this, find a new one.

Even agents who are overworked have time to make a quick phone call. If you do not hear from your agent in a week after your last meeting, find another agent.

Hard Working Agents

These are the best agents to find when you are buying your first home. If you find an agent like this one, do not lose them. These are the agents that will follow every lead, pass your wants and needs to another agent, and try their best to find you a home. You should expect to see a handful of homes when working with an agent like this one.

Now that you know more about what to look for in a real estate agent, you should feel a little more comfortable about working with one. They can be an invaluable source of information when you want to know more about homes, neighborhoods, and other questions about the communities you are looking at.

When looking at homes with your real estate agent, you should ask questions about the home, the neighborhood, the city or town, and any other questions you need to know in order to make an informed decision. Part of your real estate agent's job is to research homes and neighborhoods so that they can answer questions that may come up.

Preparing to See Homes with Your Realtor-Create a List

Once you have found a real estate agent you are comfortable with, you will want to make the most of your time when house hunting. Giving your real estate agent a list of what you are looking for will help narrow the search and save everyone some time. Your list should include:

- Your price range
- Number of bedrooms you want
- Number of bathrooms
- Size of property
- Basement (finished or unfinished)
- If you want a porch, patio, or balcony
- Central heat and air conditioning
- Garage
- Neighborhood, and
- Any other amenities you would like

Giving your real estate agent a list of your preferences will allow them to spend more time researching homes that fit the criteria. You should list these amenities from greatest to least important because no home is perfect and you will not get everything you want or need. Let your agent know that you are flexible, but that you really want to concentrate on certain items when looking for a home.

Viewing Homes

When looking at homes with your agent, be sure to ask any questions you may have. While these questions may seem small, they may be important to your happiness. Common questions people ask their agents are:

- How old is the home?
- How many owners has the home had?
- What kinds of renovations have been done to the home?
- How old is the plumbing?
- How old is the wiring?
- How old is the roof?
- How low are the sellers willing to go?
- How old is the carpeting and flooring?
- How old are the windows?

While your agent may answer some of these questions before you ask them, you should ask any questions that may influence your decision to buy a home. If you do not want to put too much work into fixing up the home, you may want to buy a home that is ten years old or less.

If your agent does not know all the answers to your questions, they should be able to find out and will give you a call within a day or two.

Taking Pictures

One of the best ways to remember the homes you have seen is to use your camera phone and take pictures. Get permission from the agent and/or home owner first before taking pictures of another person's home.

Many times, after looking at a few houses, you will forget how big the kitchen in home number two was in comparison with home number five. Having pictures will give you a better idea of the square footage and how much room you will have to work with.

Narrowing Down Your Choices

After a few weeks of viewing homes that fit what you are looking for, you should be close to finding a home that you will want to make a bid on. If you have other homes you would like to see or have changed your mind as to what you are looking for, you should tell your agent so that they can look for other homes.

Many times, if a person likes the neighborhood but not the home they were shown, they will want to see other homes in the neighborhood that are for sale. You should ask to see all of the homes available in a neighborhood that you like.

If you are still not finding a home that you like, you may need to change the neighborhoods you are looking in. While this can seem disappointing, your real estate agent will be happy to show you homes in different neighborhoods. Sometimes if you compare homes to one another, you will find redeeming qualities in a home you have already seen. Once you have found a home that you like, you should make an offer. Contact your agent as soon as you can so that they can draw up the paperwork, contact the seller's agent, and make an offer before another person does. Make an offer as soon as you can in order to avoid a bidding war.

Bidding can be long and drawn out in some cases. If you do not have the time to wait out a bid or if you cannot bid any higher, then you may be looking for another home to purchase. While this can set you back, you should try to stay positive and find a home that is right for you.

Your agent should be there to guide you along during this time. Ask all the questions you have before making an offer on a home.

Information Realtors Should Tell You

There is plenty of information that real estate agents can tell you about the homes you will be viewing. It is discriminatory if they provide certain information to one group and not to another. Things they should tell you include:

- The price of the home
- The age of the home
- Any renovations that have been done
- Any other issues with the home
- Property taxes
- Community dues
- Schools
- Neighborhood crime rates, and
- The median age of those who live in the neighborhood

Usually, if a real estate agent does not have the information you request on hand, they will be able to look it up once they are back in their office. You should be able to find out all the information you need to know in order to make an informed decision about buying a home. Realtors are required by law to give you information concerning repairs, damage, and the history of a home. This includes any incidents that have occurred inside the home such as criminal activity, fire, and other events.

You can also do a little research of your own by using the Internet, which has become a wonderful tool to use when searching for a home. You can research past events that have taken place in the neighborhood, the home itself, or the town where you want to live. Knowing a little history may prompt you to look elsewhere or make an offer.

Other information real estate agents can tell you include:

- Homeowner price reduction (your real estate agent will talk with the seller's real estate agent once you have made an offer or want to make an offer to see how low the owners will go to sell the home
- Prices of other homes in the area that are comparable to the one you are looking into buying
- How quickly the owner wants or needs to sell their home
- How much you will have to pay in property taxes each year, on average
- Other taxes in the area
- Is the home in a flood zone

Your real estate agent is a person who should be well acquainted with the neighborhoods you are looking at when buying your first home. Don't be afraid to ask many questions.

Working with Seller's and Buyer's Agent

As a home-buyer, your real estate agent is considered the buyer's agent. While some people will forego hiring an agent at first when looking for a home in order to save money on commission costs, they will usually end up hiring an agent to:

- Handle negations with seller
- Do paperwork, and
- Survey neighborhoods

It is in your best interest to hire an agent in order to make buying a home a much easier and faster process.

Negotiations with Sellers

Most people who sell their homes are also working with an agent. This agent is known as a seller's agent. If you choose not to hire an agent, you will be dealing with a seller's agent who is looking out for the home-owners' interests, and not yours.

Sometimes, though, the seller's agent and the buyer's agent can be the same agent. This means that your agent is looking after the interests of everyone involved. This is a rare occurrence, and it is best to hire a real estate agent who can negotiate with other agents in order to get you the best deal on a home.

Negotiating with agents can take a week or more depending on how high you are willing to go and how low the owners are willing to go. This can become a complicated game once you introduce home inspectors. After an initial home inspection, if you feel there are repairs that should be made prior to the sale of the home, or if you want a price reduction because of the repairs you will have to make, you will have to negotiate with the owners to settle on a fair price. Without an agent, you will have to do all of this work yourself. Why not let a pro handle that for you?

Paperwork

When buying a home, there is a lot of paperwork that must be completed before the closing. This paperwork can include:

- Offers
- Counter offers
- Home inspection reports
- Home appraisal reports, and
- Fixture lists (Items that come with the home and the items you would like removed)

Filing the paperwork is not difficult, but it can take some time. Working with an agent will save you time and money when creating and sending out various paperwork.

Survey Neighborhoods

Another advantage to hiring an agent is that you will not have to do as much legwork in the beginning. You may have a few neighborhoods in mind, but you will be able to leave it up to your agent to find homes for sale and setting up appointments to see them.

This is another time saver especially if you have to work during the week. Taking time from your busy day to call other agents and homeowners to set up appointments will distract you from your other daily duties.

Realtor Discrimination

In some cases, you may encounter a real estate professional who does not treat everyone the same. There are those that regardless of what the law says, are still practicing red lining or other discriminatory practices or disparate treatment. Unfortunately it is not easy to tell when this is happening. As was previously mentioned, a group of journalists recently uncovered the fact that 49% of interactions with real estate agents result is Black buyers being treated unequally when compared to Whites[17]. The tricky part was that the victims of this discrimination had no idea this was happening. If you feel this is happening to you it is ok to switch real estate agents. I have heard some say work with a real estate agent who looks like you. That too is a form of discrimination. It also doesn't mean an agent who looks like you isn't discriminatory. The truth is that we can't usually tell for certain when this is or isn't happening so just pay attention.

---

[17] "Undercover investigation reveals evidence of ... - Newsday." 17 Nov. 2019, https://projects.newsday.com/long-island/real-estate-agents-investigation/. Accessed 18 Jan. 2020.

More Reasons to Hire a Real Estate Agent

There are several other reasons to hire a real estate agent. These include:

Peace of Mind

The bottom line is that a buyer's agent is the best resource when it comes to finding and making an offer on a home. While a seller's agent will be able to tell you the basics about a home, they are working for the homeowner. They will not try to get you the lowest price for the home. If you enjoy negotiating, then working with the seller's agent might be for you. But, if you are like most people, hiring an agent to work on your side will make the entire process more enjoyable and worthwhile in the end.

Wealth of Knowledge

Your agent will be very knowledgeable about negotiating the right price for your new home. They will be able to help you decide where you want to live, and they will be able to guide you in buying or walking away from any property you are not sure about. This is why it is so important to talk with your agent and ask as many questions as you can before buying a home.

Confidence

If you are having doubts about purchasing the home you have made an offer on, then you should tell your agent right away so they can postpone the offer made and help you reexamine what it is you are looking for in a home. Many times the initial shock of being a homeowner can be overwhelming. Sometimes talking with your agent is enough to resolve your feelings. Other times, you may need to see a few more homes before making a decision. Your agent will be able to give you practical advice during this time.

Chapter 4 - Playing the Housing Market: Buying vs. Renting a Home

Now that you know more about finding a real estate agent, you should begin watching the housing market carefully in the weeks or months before buying your first home in order to get a feel for whether it is in your favor. This favor only changes the strategies and considerations when deciding on home buying. It should not deter you from buying just because conditions are not ideal. This would be like waiting for all the traffic lights to turn green before leaving your home to drive somewhere.

Watching the Housing Market

The real estate market cycles from a Seller's market to a Buyer's market. Depending on when you are buying, there may be more buyers than homes available or the other way around. This will impact your strategy when making offers. Ask your agent what kind of market it is and what to do about it.

This is why watching the market, surveying neighborhoods, and finding a good agent will help you in your search.

While you should not become a slave to the housing market, you should keep the following in mind before buying your first home:

- The past market value of the home you are interested in buying
- How much house your budget can get you in different neighborhoods and towns
- Neighborhood value
- How much the home should increase over time, and
- Price reductions that may be available

Just because you buy a home for a great deal does not mean you will make a huge profit when it is time to sell it. The housing market will continue to change and since this is your first home, you may want to choose something you can pay off quickly and make a larger profit on in the future.

Also, remember that many improvements you make on the home will increase its overall value. Just don't spend too much money on improvements and it is a good idea to look up which improvements give the best return. I bet you would not guess the top three correctly. Creating a home improvements budget and sticking with it will help you make those monthly mortgage payments and other payments that will be due. Some home improvements garner more value than do others. Additional square footage, kitchens and baths are among the renovations that add the most value. Some people buy their homes with these renovations in mind and use a renovation mortgage which incorporates these costs into the mortgage at the time of home purchase.

One of the biggest mistakes that the first time homeowners can make is buying a home for a lot less than they budgeted and then making improvements that will end up costing more money in the end. If you can find a great deal on a home, use that extra money as a cushion in case you lose your job or are too ill to work. Owning a home is a big responsibility. Knowing how the market is moving and spending your money wisely will help when you are creating a budget, applying for a mortgage, and deciding how much to put down on a home. Just because the bank will loan you a certain amount does not mean you should always take all they offer.

Making the Most of the Housing Market

While you should be watching the housing market, there are other areas of interest you should be watching also, such as:

- National interest rates for mortgages
- Building rates in your area
- Number of foreclosures in your area, and
- Stock market and gasoline prices

National Interest Rates for Mortgages

Even though the housing market may be going your way does not mean that the interest rates you could be paying are. In times when the housing market has taken a slump, interest rates tend to rise. When rates are low, home values seem to rise.

The interest rate you receive will depend on many factors, including:

- Other loans
- Current credit score
- Credit history

- Number of credit cards
- Yearly income
- Owed debts
- Current interest rates
- Type of lender
- Type of mortgage loan
- Type of property (1 family? 3 family? Condo?)
- Adjustable and fixed rate mortgage

If you see housing prices dropping, you may opt to buy a larger home than you would have if the prices had been higher a year ago. While you will be saving money on that end, you may be paying more each month because of the property taxes.

Building Rates in Your Area

If you notice the housing market has also caused the building of new homes in your area to decrease, then you may have to enter into a bidding war in order to buy your first home. When new home construction goes down, this can mean one of several things:

- The area is no longer popular
- The interest in buying a new home has diminished
- People can no longer afford to purchase new homes
- People are opting for older homes that are less expensive to heat and cool during the year

While that housing slump may bring a reduction of housing prices, you should consider making a bid soon after finding the home of your dreams because bidding wars will only end up costing you more money.

Number of Foreclosures in Your Area

When looking for a home, you should consider looking at homes that are foreclosed. This can be for many reasons, but usually banks that hold the titles want to unload these homes quickly so that they do not lose more money than necessary. Many times auctions will be held or the home will be advertised as a foreclosure in the newspaper or online.

There are even real estate agents who specialize in these foreclosed homes. These properties are typically called REO (it stands for real estate owned) properties. There are special considerations when buying a foreclosed home from timing on the closing to the particulars in the contract or limits to kinds of mortgages you can use when purchasing these homes. Be sure your real estate agent, lender and attorney are all familiar to the special considerations of foreclosure home buying

You should check out these homes because you may find exactly what you are looking for in a home. In many cases that ugly beat up home can be a diamond in the rough. Many people use various types of renovation mortgage loans to buy these homes and turn them into what they truly desire.

Stock Market and Gasoline Prices

Even if you do not play the stock market game or own a car, you should still pay attention to these areas because they usually have an impact on housing prices and the cost to heat and cool the home.

When the stock market is doing well, many people will spend their money freely, which will give way to higher housing prices. But, when gasoline prices go up, so will the price to heat and cool a home, which may make home buyers reconsider buying until prices fall again.

This could be a good time to buy a home if you are willing to pay a little more each month in utility costs.

The impact society can have on the housing market can be huge, and it can also have lasting effects. Buyer's markets are created when there are more homes available than buyers, while seller's market occurs when there are more people who want to purchase homes than there are for sale. These housing markets go back and forth due to issues mentioned above.

In the End

In the end, when you are ready to buy a home, you should make the decision based on what you can afford and how much money you can put down for your new home. Just because you find a home that has a huge price reduction and you are comfortable financially, does not mean you must buy that home.

Buy a home when you are ready. Many times, people will buy a home because it is cheaper in the long run than paying rent each month. The downside to home ownership is that you have to make your mortgage payments on time each month. Very few lenders will give you more time to come up with the money. If you miss even one payment, you may begin the slide down the slippery slope of foreclosure because once you miss one or two payments most find it quite difficult to catch up. You will have no place to live and your credit score will suffer severely. This is why having a reserve fund or an emergency fund is so critical. It is even more critical if your familial network won't be able to help you out in a bind.

If you can afford to make the move into your new home, you should not wait too long before making an offer. The housing market can change quickly and with competition out there, you may end up losing more money if you don't make an offer after seeing a home that you like.

Buying vs. Renting (Pros/Cons)

Even though in the long run, buying a home is more cost effective than renting a home because of the equity that will build up over time, many people are just not comfortable carrying the weight of paying for a home on their shoulders. Also, those who have to travel often for work may not want the day to day upkeep that owning a home requires.

There are plenty of pros and cons when it comes to buying a home versus renting a home. Since you are thinking about buying your first home, you should consider these pros and cons for several reasons. First, if you are currently renting a home, you may want to invest in property that you can later sell. Second, you will be responsible for repairs and maintenance for the home instead of being able to call your landlord or maintenance crew. The third reason you should weigh the pros and cons is if you are planning to move in the next few years. If the housing market is a buyer's market for now, you may have difficulty selling the home later on.

Buying a Home
Pros
- Investment property – value will hopefully only increase or remain the same
- Build equity that you can use later on
- You can improve upon your home any way you want
- You can decorate it to suit your needs
- No landlord or property management company
- Sense of stability
- The average homeowner has over 40 times the net worth of the average renter (yes forty times!) [18]
- Ability to live in a community, and
- You have something to sell later on

Cons
- You are responsible for all repair and maintenance costs
- Monthly payments for utilities and mortgage are more expensive
- Could take time to sell later on

Renting a Home
Pros
- You are not responsible for repairs and maintenance costs
- You are free to leave once the lease has expired
- In many cases, utilities are being paid by the landlord

[18] "The Net Worth of a Homeowner is 44x Greater Than A Renter ...." 20 Aug. 2018, https://www.keepingcurrentmatters.com/en/2018/08/20/the-net-worth-of-a-homeowner-is-44x-greater-than-a-renter/. Accessed 18 Jan. 2020.

- Many apartment buildings have some sort of security system
- Sometimes less expensive than paying a monthly mortgage
- Credit score is unaffected if rent cannot be paid on time

Cons
- Privacy issues
- May have to share washers and dryers
- Rent to be increased once lease expires
- Landlord may not fix items on time
- Cannot paint walls or add other features
- Deposit may be required
- May not allow pets
- Neighbors come and go
- You are not accumulating net worth at the rate of homeowners
- African-Americans are charged more for rent in many neighborhoods than Whites [19]

As you can see, there are many factors that you should consider when thinking about buying your first home.

If you are ready financially and want to have your own space, you should find an agent and start looking. The average time that most people take to make an offer on a home once they start looking is two weeks. If you have not found a home within that time, you should either continue looking or rethink your strategy. Talk with your real estate agent and decide what you may want to

---

[19] "Analysis: African-Americans pay more for rent, especially in ...." 31 Oct. 2018, https://www.chicagoreporter.com/analysis-african-americans-pay-more-for-rent-especially-in-white-neighborhoods/. Accessed 18 Jan. 2020.

change if anything. Do we need to look at a different price point or neighborhood ? Are our offers too slow or too low? Should you begin looking at foreclosures or stop looking at foreclosures? Are your expectations realistic?

Rent to Own

Another option you may have is to buy the property you are currently renting or rent a property that also offers you the option to buy after a certain amount of time. This will give you a chance to see if you like living in the home and will give you time to get your finances in order.

Rent to own properties are usually older than other homes and have been rental properties for some time. This means that they may not be in great shape. If you are looking for a property that you don't mind repairing, then this option may be for you.

When looking for a rent to own property, you should ask the following questions:

- · How old is the home?
- · How many times has it been rented out?
- · What is the mortgage payment on the home?
- · What is the rent per month for the home?
- · How long will I have to make my decision?
- · What happens if I change my mind?

You should still sign the proper contracts stating that you are interested in buying the home after a given time period. This will protect your rights and the rights of the current homeowner.

New Homes

When you think of your first home, you may be thinking of a brand new home. If the housing market is favoring buyers at the moment, you may get a great deal from a builder that is developing a new housing community, or you may find a plot of land that is in an existing community. This can be a great alternative to buying an older home for many reasons:

- You will have a part in designing the home
- You will have new appliances and lighting fixtures
- You will have new carpeting and flooring
- You will be able to choose all of the fixtures, carpeting, and flooring
- You will be able to add a porch or a patio, and
- You will be able to place the home where you want it on your property.

A new home can be very exciting, but it can also be a lot of extra work. The first step in buying a new home is to find property. You should visit builders and real estate agents who will file all of the necessary paperwork, permits, and other items needed to build on the property. This can take a few weeks, so be sure to plan accordingly.

The next step is to design the home. This is the fun part where you will get to personalize your home to suit your needs.

Once you have been approved for a mortgage, the property has passed all of the land inspections, and the home has been designed, construction will begin. Depending on the time of year, you will have to wait months or even a year before you can move into your new home.

After construction is complete, you should complete a walkthrough of the home, check all of the fixtures, and have the home inspected before signing the final paperwork. Then the home is yours.

Many people hire a lawyer during the construction phase so that all of the paperwork has been filed and there are no problems during the walkthrough.

Buying a new home is just one more option you should consider when looking for your first home. Home construction can vary as there are a few ways to build a home, including prefabricated ("prefab") homes that will be built elsewhere and delivered to your property where they will be assembled. Look into all of your options before deciding on a home that is right for you and your budget.

Using the Housing Market to Your Advantage

By paying attention to the current housing trends and keeping a watchful eye on the homes in our area, you will be able to make an offer on a home that will be accepted. While the market is continually changing, it is a useful tool for those who are on a budget, who want to find a home that is large enough to suit their needs, and will be worth more when it is time to sell it.

When watching the housing market, consider the following:

- The number of homes that are in your area

- The number of days the homes have been on the market
- The price of a new home compared to those that are being sold by homeowners
- The price of renting vs. buying
- The number of homes that are in your price range
- The highest price you can pay when buying a home
- Interest rates in comparison to housing prices, and
- The time of year

When to Buy

Many people believe the Spring is the best time. There are usually many homes coming to the market. Sometimes families want to sell in the spring and close when their children get out of school and use the summer to relocate. Homes do move the fastest during the spring and the first part of summer. Some don't want to show their homes during the Winter if one lives in an area with challenging weather conditions.

Some prefer the late summer or fall when there is less competition and some of those spring sellers are now more eager to sell which could mean a better negotiations or concessions. They may cut prices so they can move before school starts up again or the bad weather impedes their sale. Homeowners that need to sell their homes before a certain time are more willing to reduce the price of their homes.

The reality is that the best and/or worst time to buy may depend on where you live. There may not be an ideal time. The best time to buy is when you are ready.

While the housing market can change, the idea of selling one's home will not. Homeowners may choose to wait out the current housing market, but if they are eager to buy another home or move to a new place, their wait will be short-lived. Negotiate with homeowners until a fair price can be reached. This is the same practice during a seller's market as in a buyer's market. You may have to play the bidding game for a week or two, but in the end, it is the person who needs to make the transaction happen the most that will end up compromising the most.

Chapter 5 - Home Inspections

A home inspection will give you a chance to discover more about the home before you purchase it. In case there are serious problems with the foundation, mold issues, or underground leaks, you will be prepared to ask for repairs, a reduced price, or walk away from the property.

The Importance of Home Inspections

Finding a home does not mean that your investigative duties are over. Although most states do not have required inspections, your lender may require at the very least a pest inspection that will need to be conducted before they agree to approve your mortgage loan. If there are termites or other insects, the homeowners will have to take care of the problem before they sell the home.

But what about full home inspections? Are they worth it? In most cases, the answer is yes. Although you will have to pay for a home inspection, it may save you a lot of money in the long run.

A thorough home inspection will include checking the following:

- Electrical systems
- Heating and cooling systems
- Foundation
- Siding
- Structural elements

- Roof
- Insulation
- Doors and windows, and
- Plumbing

If you are buying a new or used home, it is best to have a home inspection before signing the final paperwork. Once the inspection report comes back, you will have the opportunity to ask the homeowners for a price reduction, go ahead and buy the home anyway, or ask the homeowners to make the necessary repairs.

You will have a varied reaction from homeowners. Many times, they will agree to lower the price a little.

When drawing up the initial offer for the purchase of the home, you should include a statement that allows you to withdraw your bid if any repairs are not taken care of or the price is not lowered due to the findings by the home inspector. If the contract does not include this, then you can still withdraw from the bid, but you may owe the agent commission fees. Ask your attorney about this standard clause.

Having a home inspection will give you peace of mind when you are buying a home. Since you will be taking out a mortgage, it is important to know what you will be buying, and the amount of money you will have to invest after purchasing the home. A home inspection will also help you make your final decision whether to purchase the home or to keep looking for another.

How to Find a Home Inspector

There are a few places to turn when looking for a home inspector:

- Your real estate agent
- Your mortgage lender
- References from friends and family

- The phone book, and
- Contractors

Ask around and see if you can get references of other homeowners that will give you a good report. Many home inspectors work freelance and only work certain days during the week. They are trained in home inspection and many are retired contractors, builders, electricians, and plumbers who know what they are looking for.

When you find a few home inspectors, give them a call and ask the following questions:
- How long have you been inspecting homes?
- How much do you charge per hour?
- What do you look for when inspecting a home?
- What types of reports should I expect?
- What days during the week are you available?
- Do you offer septic system inspections?
- What type of licensing do you have?

A thorough home inspection should take an inspector about three hours to complete. This will give you an idea of how much the inspection will cost.

Once you have asked these questions, find out if your lender has specific inspections that the home must pass before you will receive a home loan. If the inspector can complete these inspections along with the home inspection, then it is worth the time and money to have the inspector complete all the inspections on the same day.

The next step after choosing an inspector and finding out which inspections will be needed by your lender is to make sure the homeowners will be home for the inspection. Usually your agent will arrange a time for the inspector to perform the inspection.

It is up to you if you would like to be present for the inspection or not. Many times, the reports will be enough to give you a clear idea of what needs to be done. After the inspection is complete and the reports have been completed, it is up to the homeowners to either make the repairs necessary or lower their asking price.

If the repairs are minor and will not require too much money to repair, they will usually agree to make the repairs. If you would like to absorb the cost of the repairs, then you can offer to do so. You should receive this decision in writing so that there is no confusion during the final walkthrough before the closing. At the closing, you should have all of your paperwork, including the home inspection reports with you in case there is a discrepancy.

What to Expect from a Home Inspection

A home inspection can unearth many problems you did not notice during your visits to the home. Typical findings include:

- Crumbling foundation
- Structural damage to floors, walls and ceilings
- Water damage inside and outside the walls
- Termite damage
- Porch railings or posts in poor condition
- Heating and cooling systems need to be cleaned or do not work properly
- Roof needs repair
- Sinkholes
- Broken or leaking pipes
- Electrical wiring not functioning or broken

- Broken water fixtures or light fixtures
- Windows that do not open
- Uneven doorways
- Improper insulation
- Mold
- Water contamination
- Septic tank issues, or
- Hazardous chemicals

Most homes will only experience a few minor issues, but some older homes may have more problems than they are worth. The damage to the homes could cost you thousands of dollars if you are unaware of the damage prior to purchasing the home. While disclosure of some problems is mandatory, many homeowners do not even know that some of these problems exist until they try to sell their homes.

On the day of the inspection, you should expect to hear about some of the problems. You should be given a detailed report of the findings that will outline drastic problems and those that can be fixed easily.

Some lenders will not approve the home loan until the problems are fixed and another inspection is conducted.

Specific Places that Should be Inspected

When interviewing home inspectors, make sure to ask whether the following areas are inspected:

- Chimney and fireplace
- Attic and basement
- Crawl space
- Swimming pools, and

· Smoke detectors and appliances

These are important areas that can be very costly to repair once you have purchased the home. Many homeowners are willing to replace a chimney cap or remove mold from the basement. You should make sure that these areas are inspected prior to the closing. You should also inspect these areas during the final walkthrough.

Chimney and Fireplace

Inspectors should be looking for:

- Missing, broken, or intact chimney caps
- Mortar between chimneys is intact
- Metal chimneys are not bent or contain holes and have all screws in place
- Creosote – this is buildup caused from wood burning fireplaces, and is flammable if not removed

Attic, Basement, and Crawl Spaces

Home inspectors should be on the lookout for the following:

- Mold
- Fire damage
- Rotting beams
- Insulation
- Damage from water, and
- Damage from animals and pests

Swimming Pools

When looking at the swimming pool, the inspector should look at the following:

- Swimming pool plumbing, and
- Swimming pool shell

Smoke Detectors and Appliances

- Make sure they work
- No leaks
- Check for broken hoses or connections
- Broken door handles
- Inadequate wiring

Termite Inspection

A termite inspection is a separate inspection that will give you an idea of structural damage to the home that has been caused by termites and other pests. This inspection is required by most lenders before they will guarantee you the money to purchase the home.

Termite inspections are not covered under the standard fee of a home inspection, so you may have to pay for the inspection unless the homeowners are willing to do so.

The inspection should take about an hour and will entail the inspector looking underneath the siding, in basements, attics, and on the foundation of the home to see if there are termites present or if there are other insects such as ants, or fungus that are destroying the wood. The inspector will also conduct an inspection inside the home as well. Since termites can live in different weather conditions, you should have the inspection done even if you live in an area that has lower temperatures than other regions. Termites are prevalent where I live and the termite report is standard.

Termites can be removed using an insecticide that is specially designed to kill termites and their eggs, but the damage left behind can be immense. If the home has been infested for a long time, then it may be beyond repair.

You will then have to discuss a reduction in price, repairs being made to the property, or walking away altogether.

How Homeowners Will React

How the homeowner will react to the results of the home inspection could determine whether you continue pursuing the home or whether you let it go and find another one.

Homeowners have their own agenda when it comes to selling their home. These include:
- Buying another home
- Moving to another state
- Using the money to pay for family medical emergencies
- Retirement, or
- Making money on an investment property

This means that there are varying degrees as to what they are willing to pay for and what they are not willing to pay for. If the homeowner is not in a rush to sell, then they may contest the findings and refuse to repair certain items. If they need to make as much money as possible, they may agree to lower the price a little or make repairs that cost the least on the list.

You will have to make some tough decisions at this point. If the repairs will be needed on the home are required by the lender, you can:

- Try to find another lender
- Try to get the homeowners to pay for the repairs
- Include the repairs in your loan (renovation type loans)
- Pay for the repairs yourself, or
- Walk away from the home

Whichever decision you make, you will have to live with the consequences.

Homeowners know they are taking risks when selling older homes. But what about new homes? If your new home does not pass inspection, it is up to the builder to make the necessary repairs. You should make sure this is included in the contract before signing it.

If you are buying a home that the homeowners have already moved out of, you may be able to get the repairs paid for without having to be too pushy. If the homeowners are paying another mortgage, they are eager to sell and may opt to pay for the repairs upfront or give you a price reduction. This will depend on the circumstances. There is always a certain amount of luck that goes into buying a home.

Ways a Home Inspection Can Lower the Final Price

Even though you will have to spend money upfront for a home inspection, you may save more money than you anticipated once the results come back. This is especially true for older homes or new homes that were not built using the right materials or according to safety codes.

There are a few ways you will be able to negotiate a lower price on the home before signing the final contracts.

- Ask homeowners to make repairs

This is the best way to save money on your new home. While you will not see a reduction in the final price of the home, you will not have to make as many repairs down the road. Also, you will not have to worry about the repairs once you have moved into the home.

While all homeowners are different, you should be aware that many do not want to make repairs unless the home absolutely cannot be sold in the condition it is in because it will endanger the new owners. Even minor repairs may pose a problem for homeowners. You should be firm, but friendly when negotiating this part of the contract. If you do not want to make these repairs and you strongly feel that the repairs should be made by the homeowner, you can still walk away from the home and find another.

You should give the homeowners a week to think about making the repairs. Most homeowners will make their decision quickly because they want the sale to go through.

- ## Ask homeowners for a price reduction

If the homeowners do not want to spend money on the repairs that you have requested, they may agree to drop the final price of the home. While the price reduction will not be too drastic, any reduction is good since you will have to make the repairs yourself down the road.

If the homeowners suggest a reduction in the final price, you should consider the offer and find out how much the repairs will cost you. If it seems like a fair deal, then take it. If not, you can always ask for a larger reduction. Most buyers and sellers eventually agree on a price that will suit both parties.

- ## Ask homeowners to pay for all/some closing costs

Another way to save money without relying on the homeowners to pay for the repairs is if they agree to pay the closing costs on both sides. This will free up some of your money so that you can make the repairs yourself.

You may have to have a separate contract drawn up that will explain what the homeowners are responsible for paying, and what you are responsible for paying. This will make buying the home much easier.

Any agreements that you make with the homeowners should be made in writing. Verbal agreements do not stand up in court, and are not common practice among real estate lawyers and agents when they are closing a deal. Your agent should make this clear to you at the beginning of the home buying process.

Do not be discouraged if there seems to be a lot of paperwork. This is necessary and the usual standard practice for those who want to protect themselves from wrongdoing and lawsuits later on.

The Final Walkthrough

On the day of the closing, you should have a final walkthrough whether you are purchasing a new home or an older home. Final walkthroughs are a way for you to determine if there is anything else you will need to discuss, get in writing, or have changed before you sign the paperwork.

The final walkthrough will include you, the homeowners, real estate agents, and if necessary, your lawyer. Unfortunately, many buyers skip the final walkthrough in anticipation of moving into the home quickly. But you should have one more walkthrough just to be sure.

The benefits of a final walkthrough include:

- Making sure all repairs that were conceded by the homeowners have been made
- Be sure additional repairs are not necessary
- Walls are intact
- Plumbing is intact
- Flush toilets in the home
- Garage door opener
- Test doors and windows
- All appliances that were remaining are still in the home
- Appliances are in good working condition
- Electrical systems are working by turning on all lights

- All junk is removed from the yard as per prior agreements

You will feel much better after the final walkthrough for many reasons. You will get to see first-hand the repairs that have been made, you will begin to see yourself living in the home, and you will be able to plan for the future in terms of what you want to keep in the home and what you want to remove.

In some cases, you will never meet the homeowners. If they have moved before putting the house on the market, you may be dealing directly with the homeowner's lawyer. It is still a good idea to ask questions about the home before signing the final paperwork.

The Closing

The closing is your last chance to ask for changes to the contract, to bring any concerns, and to ask the homeowners any questions you may have about the home and the property.

At the closing, you should bring:

- A notepad
- Financial notes and mortgage approval paperwork
- Signed paperwork you have received over the course of the deal
- Identification, and
- The home inspection report

At this meeting, you will be signing the paperwork that will make the home yours. This is a very exciting time, but you should maintain your composure to make sure that you are getting what you are signing for. If repairs have not been made, then you have the option to wait until they are complete.

When to Walk Away

Any time after the home inspection if you begin to have doubts about purchasing the home, you should contact your real estate agent and voice your concerns. Don't over react however. Remember that the job of the inspector is to find what is wrong with the home so they will find something. No home is going to be perfect and without a single issue or flaw. Many first time home buyers need reassurance that they are making the right decisions. Your real estate agent will want the sale to go through, but they know that there are other properties they can show you, so they are not really losing money if you decide not to buy the home.

There are many reasons to walk away from a home sale. These include:

- A bad report from the home inspector
- The homeowners are unwilling to pay for necessary repairs
- You find another home that suits your needs
- The price for the home is too high
- You decide you don't like the neighborhood
- Loss of your job, or
- A medical emergency

Walking away from a specific home is not giving up on your dream of ownership. Unfortunately, there are times in life when buying a home is not possible. If the financial strain is going to be too much, for example, then you should seriously consider finding a lower priced home or a smaller home.

If you decide to walk away from a home, you should give yourself a few days to recuperate before going out there and finding another home. You should contact:

- The real estate agent
- The lender, or
- The builder

Let them know of your decision and that you will be in touch when the time is right. Many times, after a bad report from a home inspector, it is just not worth spending the money on a home that will require a lot of repairs down the road. While all older homes will have some repairs, you should know the limits of what is acceptable and what will cost you too much money.

If you can get enough financing and you want to pursue the home regardless of the repairs that will have to be made, then go for it. Sometimes buying an older home and fixing it up can be a fun activity for everyone involved. Only you can make these crucial decisions. A home inspection will help you realize how much work and money may be involved if you decide to purchase the home.

When to NOT walk away

Again: don't over react. All homes have issues. Realize the inspector job is to find them and then you decide how to deal with them. If the seller's are willing to negotiate you may be able to make the deal work. If there are safety issues, the lender will likely require those be fixed to ensure the home is safe to live in. The seller can fix them or you can use special loans like renovation loans, to include the repairs in the loan and have the repairs done after closing. Get a bid from a contractor to show the cost and use this in the negotiations. Keep in mind that beyond the cost of the work is your time and inconvenience which also has a cost. What if you can't occupy the home for a period of time and need to pay rent elsewhere?

If the issues are not safety related you may be able to close and fix them later or maybe on your own if you have the skills to do the work. In my opinion I prefer to negotiate many repairs off the price and handle them myself. My belief is that a seller fixing a home they are leaving won't care about the quality of repair the same way the person buying the home will care.

Remember nearly everything is negotiable so if the house is a fit, the neighborhood is a fit, the price is a fit, find a reasonable way to make it work.

Chapter 6 - Financing Your First Home

Financing your first home can be the most frustrating part of the home buying process. This is the time when you will figure out how to pay for the home. Most people have to take out a mortgage loan in order to afford the price. Which mortgage loans are right for you? How much of a down payment will be necessary? What is escrow? What are closing costs?

You will have many questions about financing your first home. By knowing the facts, paying attention to interest rates, and looking into all of your mortgage options, you will be able to choose repayment terms that will fit your current income and allow you to safely make those monthly payments.

Types of Home Loans

Deciding which home loan is the right one for you will depend on what you qualify for and what your lender is willing to give you. There are a few types of mortgage loans, including:

- Fixed rate mortgage loans
- Adjustable rate mortgage loans
- Balloon mortgages, and
- Jumbo loans
- Renovation loans
- VA Loans
- FHA Loans

- Conventional Loans
- Non-QM

You should be familiar with these loans so that you will be able to make an informed decision when it comes to financing your new home.

Fixed Rate Mortgage Loans

For the vast majority of home buyers and for most first time home buyers who are on a strict budget, choosing a fixed rate mortgage may be the best loan for you. Your monthly payment will never change for the life of the loan because you will lock into the interest rate given at the time the loan was processed. You can take out loans that range from ten to thirty years.

There are many advantages to taking out mortgage loans that have fixed rates. You will be able to create a monthly budget for yourself, you will never be surprised by the amount you will have to pay each month, and you will be able to lock into a low interest rate.

The disadvantages may not mean much to you now, but as your family or your income grows, you may want to refinance and pay less each month so that you will be able to afford renovations, vacations, and other luxuries. Since your mortgage is fixed, if interest rates drop, you will be paying a higher rate. While you can refinance your mortgage, this comes with a cost.

Usually when rates are low it is a good idea to lock into a fixed rate. When interest rates are high the adjustable rate loans become attractive as they can adjust downwards when rates fall again

For those who have limited income, who have lower credit scores, or those who want the security of paying the same amount each month, then a fixed rate mortgage is the loan for you.

Adjustable Rate Mortgage Loans

If you expect to make more money in the next few years, and want to buy a bigger home, you may be interested in an adjustable rate mortgage. The major difference between an adjustable rate mortgage and a fixed rate mortgage is that the interest rate will vary year to year in an adjustable rate mortgage. When rates are high this future adjustment may result n a lower rate and reduced payments.

While the interest will be capped, you will still be paying more for each year that you own your home unless interest rates drop over an extended period of time. Most adjustable rate mortgages cannot be raised more than 1 or 2 interest points per year, and up to 5 points maximum for the life of the loan. Ask about the particulars of the loan being offered to you.

These loans are good for those who want a larger home and who expect to increase their earnings each year to afford the increase. If you are in a position to take out an adjustable rate mortgage, you will be able to lock into a fixed rate that may be lower than your original rate. This is the main advantage of these loans.

Be sure to carefully discuss and consider both the short term and long term impact of an adjustable rate loan. When rates are low it is usually best to avoid the ARM and take a fixed.

Balloon Mortgages

If you are only planning on living in your first home for a few years (usually five to seven), you could look into a balloon mortgage. These mortgages require that you pay them off in five to seven years. They have a lower interest rate that is fixed.

If, after the term of the mortgage has passed and you want to remain in the home, you will have to refinance and choose a fixed rate or adjustable rate mortgage to pay off the existing mortgage, as balloon mortgages cannot be renewed.

Only consider this mortgage if you are planning on moving after a certain amount of time or if you think you can pay the mortgage off in that amount of time.

Jumbo Loans

Most first time home buyers will not need to take out a jumbo loan unless they are buying a very large home. These loans are valued over $726,525 (this number usually changes each year and varies around the country from county to county - this is the 2020 number) and are used to purchase land and a home. More collateral will be needed in order to qualify for one of these loans. The interest rates are comparable to fixed and adjustable rate mortgages and have the same payment terms.

Renovation loans

These loans allow you to include money in your mortgage for renovations or repairs to the home. These are frequently used when buying distressed properties, older homes, damaged short sales properties or foreclosures. The home is not required to be in poor condition however.

When buying a distressed home or damaged home or foreclosure frequently the lender will not usually allow you to close if the house doesn't have functioning utilities, has any issues that could be a health or safety concerns to the occupants or is missing things you would expect to find in a standard home (like missing toilets or windows). The renovation loan is a way to bypass this issue as you can fix these things or have them fixed after closing.

Many first time home buyers find themselves spending most or all available funds to get into the home. The renovation loan allows you to include funds for that kitchen renovation or new bathroom right into the mortgage. The benefit is that this is at mortgage rates, spread over the life of the loan (likely 30 years) and the interest is tax deductible in the same way interest on any other home loan is tax deductible. For most homebuyers this beats buying the home and then putting the renovations on the high interest credit card.

Another strategy to use with the renovation loan when housing inventory in your desired area is limited is to look for homes below your price range with the intent of renovating the home into what you want. Location, location, location is what's important. A renovation loan can fix or change anything else. Some people buy a 3 bedroom ranch and turn it into a 5 bedroom colonial if the location is right. Others look for that home with the dated kitchen and bathrooms and put the renovations in their budget. For example rather than buy a $450,000 home one could buy a $400,000 home and have $50,000 to renovate it. Of course the values of the home have to make sense. In other words you wouldn't be able to buy a $400,000 home with $50,000 in renovations if the after completed value would only be $400,000. The after improved value must justify the transaction.

The renovation loans overlap with the loan types above and below. There are renovation loans that are FHA or VA or Conventional. Some are Fixed or Adjustable. The renovation loan attributes can overlap with the other loan types

VA loans

VA stands for Veterans Affairs (not Virginia!). This is short for the U.S. Department of Veterans Affairs. It is a department within the Federal Government. The VA helps service members, veterans and eligible survivors become homeowners. They have 0% down programs and a few other benefits. If you are within one of the categories above it would make sense to see if you are eligible and if the benefits offered are of value to you.

FHA loans

FHA loans are insured by the Federal Housing Administration. They offer loans that are frequently used by first time home buyers but are available to more than just first timers.

This kind of loan is more forgiving than other types when it comes to mediocre to poor credit. It also has a low down payment requirement, allows for gifts from family and has a few other features that make it attractive to first time home buyers (more forgiving with less than stellar credit scores, allows use of income for qualifying purposes when buying a multi-family property, and more)

Conventional loans

These are the "vanilla" plain loan typically. Conventional loans are normally those loans backed by Fannie Mae or Freddi Mac. Those are the quasi-governmental institutions that provide the banks with the money they lend. In many cases the banks are lending money from this source. Yes even "direct" lenders.

Non-QM loans

QM stands for "Qualified Mortgage". A QM Mortgage is a defined class of mortgages that meet certain borrower and lender standards as defined in the Dodd-Frank Regulation of 2010. This regulation made certain loans like no income check or no document loans nearly extinct. There are still Non-QM loans available in the marketplace. They are not as prevalent, they are typically more expensive and restrictive, and they don't allow for all that was available before 2010.

Now that you know about the types of mortgages that are available, you should be thinking about which lender to use. With so many lenders out there, it may be difficult to sort through all of them and find the right one. Doing a little homework will help you get the best fit.

Where to Find a Lender

These days there are many places to find a mortgage lender, such as:

- Family or friends
- Your attorney
- Your real estate agent
- Your current lender

As you can see, finding a lender should not be too difficult. You may have to contact several lenders before you find a lender that will give you a loan that meets your needs. When you apply for a home mortgage loan, the lender will check the following:

- Your credit score
- Your credit history
- Your current income
- Income of a co-signer, if necessary
- Current interest rates based on the amount you are requesting
- Status of other loans you may have
- Number of years you have been eligible to work, and
- Number of years you have had credit

There are many factors that will go into your approval or denial of a home loan. You will have to be patient. Be sure your lender is exposing the process so you grasp what is happening and how long it takes.

You should feel free to contact your lender at any time during the home buying process with questions and concerns you may have. Other important information the lender will need before granting you a loan include:

- The home inspection report
- The termite inspection report, and
- The home appraisal report

These reports are very important to a lender because they will tell the lender how much the home is actually worth and the types of damage that have lowered the overall value of the property. Lenders expect homeowners to remain in the home for at least five years. This will allow them to make a profit on the money they have loaned you. It is not worth it to them if you have to sell the home shortly after buying it because there is too much damage and you can no longer live there.

Online Lenders

Many people ask about online lenders in today's internet world. The online lenders do differ from your local lender or even the national bank with a local presence. These differences may or may not be important to you.

Your local lender is likely to have a level of accountability to your local real estate agent, especially if the lender was recommended by that agent. If the local lender creates a bad reputation or performs poorly, that real estate agent may not refer them any longer or may share the poor performance with others and impact that lenders ability to do business. This means the lender is very concerned about you as a borrower. Your relationship with the lender is an extension of the relationship the lender has developed with the real estate agent. They will fight hard to keep that intact. The online lender as a company has a broader perspective and is not likely to be as concerned about your corner of the world or your real estate agent. If your loan doesn't work out or you get denied late in the process because your online lender missed something you don't get to rate their performance since you didn't close. This may happen more than you think. For this to happen to your referred lender could be catastrophic so they will avoid this at all costs.

Consider what the online lender is offering. Most of their advertisements mention you can get your pre-approval fast and it is available 24 hours a day. Why do you need a mortgage at 2 a.m.? Why do you need it fast? If you need your pre-approval on the same day you begin home shopping that is called poor planning. Since you are reading this book that is not you. Buying a home is for most people, the biggest financial transaction of their lives. Doesn't it make sense to take your time and do it correctly rather than rush it? If you answered yes, then 24 hour availability and being approved in 5 minutes or less is not necessary.

Some of the online lenders can be more expensive as well. Guess who paid for that SuperBowl ad and all those commercials? Revenue from the consumer. When you buy the largest SUV on the market you don't expect it to have the best gas mileage as well. You understand that there are tradeoffs. The same applies to your chosen lender. If you want the convenience you will pay for it. Do you do your regular food shopping at the local 24 hour convenience store?

You can also ask the other parties in your transaction (your real estate agent, your attorney) about their experiences with any particular online lender. They may have additional insight not mentioned here.

Applying for a Home Loan

When applying for a home loan, you will have to bring the following information to the lender's office, or if applying online, supply copies that are faxed to the lender or emailed or uploaded into their system. What you will need to provide:

- 2 years of tax returns (all pages)
- 2 years of W2 forms
- Your most recent paycheck stub
- 2 months of bank statements (all pages)
- 2 recent 401K statements (if applicable) all pages
- Government issued photo identification

You will be asked additional questions that will help the lenders determine if you are able to pay the loan back on time. These questions include:

- Number of years renting a home or apartment
- Late payment on credit cards and other loans
- Active loans (such as student loans or car loans)
- Number of years at your current job
- Additional income
- Amount of the loan and number of years to pay it back
- Number of years living in an area
- Dependents that are living in your home
- Tax returns and bank statements

Applying for a loan can take a week or more. This is because background checks, credit checks, and references must be checked before the loan will be processed. Review of all of your information may also raise new questions which require further documentation or clarification. This is normal and should not alarm you.

In the meantime, you should be concentrating on gathering your paperwork and sorting through your papers in case you cannot find everything the lender requests.

If you do not have your back tax returns, you can contact the IRS and request them by year. Many times, lenders will need to see returns from at least three years ago. Bank statements and bill statements from the past year should be enough to secure a loan.

If you are turned down for a home loan, you will be notified as to the reasons why. This can be devastating, but you should find other lenders and try to apply again. If you have poor credit, you may need to go through a lender that specializes in granting loans to those with poor credit. You may have to pay a higher interest rate, but at least you will be granted a loan.

Reasons for possible denial include:

- Poor credit or not enough credit
- Length of time at your job is too short
- Income level for the amount of loan requested
- Loan default
- Failure to pay rent or other bills, or
- Too much debt

Applying for a home loan can be stressful, but if you have good credit, steady employment, and enough income, you should have little trouble qualifying for a loan.

What Not to do When Applying for a Home Loan

There are a few things you should not do after applying for a home loan:

- Finance a new car
- Begin a new job without discussing with the lender
- Co-signing for someone else's loan
- Close credit accounts or credit cards
- Buy new furniture or other large items using your credit cards
- Take out new loans or finance new things in general
- Apply for a credit card, or
- Default on student loans or other loans

All of these actions will cause your credit score to change that will give lenders an inaccurate view of your spending habits and your overall credit score. If you take a job that pays you less than you noted on your home loan application, your lender may not agree to grant you the loan. If you change from W2 to self-employed, your lender may not be able to grant you the loan. If you change from salary to commission, your lender may not be able to grant you the loan. Don't make these changes without a conversation first.

If possible, do not begin a new job until you have moved into your home. Try not to spend money on credit cards. Buy furniture and other items using cash, or wait until you have signed the final contract and are a homeowner.

The general rule is really pretty simple. Your lender has approved you based on a profile of information. Your income amount and source, your credit history and amount of financial obligation, your current asset profile, etc. When you change these things, you can change your ability to be approved. Just check with your lender during the loan process before making any changes. By the way "I just quit my job, does that?" doesn't count as checking with your lender.

How Much Can I Afford

While there are many items that will change this number, the most important answer is, do you have a budget? Most first time buyers have never put together a real budget. Use the following two forms to answer this question of what can you REALLY afford. The short answer lenders look for is what is called Debt to Income ratio or DTI. The second form will show you what your DTI will allow. For some loans your DTI should not exceed 43% or 50% or even 56%. This can vary by loan type and by lender. While that statement might seem scary and technical, the following forms will make this a very simple math problem.

BUDGET

INCOME SOURCE	INCOME
Borrower Gross Income	
Co-Borrower Gross Income	
TOTAL GROSS INCOME	
TOTAL NET INCOME	
EXPENSE DESCRIPTION	**AMOUNT**
Rent	
Food	
Utilities (gas, water, electric, trash)	
Gasoline	
Cell Phone & Land Line	
Home Maintenance	
Dry Cleaning	
Housekeeper	
Child Care	
Visa, Master Card, Dept. Store payments	
Car Payments	
TOTAL EXPENSES	

TOTAL NET INCOME	
TOTAL EXPENSES	
EQUALS ABILITY TO SAVE	

Now consider this: what the bank says they will lend you is not the same as what you can afford. Realize the bank is approving you for a number that allows them to get paid back. They don't know if you are saving for retirement or if you have expensive hobbies or children's activities. You decide what you can afford. However don't do what we see too often. Some people decide on the payment they can afford and then pick a neighborhood or home that is beyond that budget and then try to make it fit. If your budget will allow you to buy a $300,000 home don't go to a $600,000 and "low-ball" thinking you will find a desperate person who would like to sell their home at half-price.

Increase Your Chances for Approval

There are a few ways to increase your chances for loan approval that will also help you determine what you will be able to afford each month:

· Pre-approval

Many experts agree that applying for a loan before you find a home and being pre-approved will help you create a budget, buy a home that is in your price range, and help lenders make their decisions faster. Get the best, strongest, most detailed pre-approval you can. Don't settle for a lender who gives you a quick letter without a credit check and full review of your documents.

- Ask for only the amount you will need

One way to increase your chances for a home loan is to not ask for more than you will qualify for. This means you will have to look at your income level, the amount of debt you have, and the expected monthly mortgage expenses, because your lender will. Apply for the amount you will need and nothing more.

- Pay off credit cards

If you are thinking about buying a home in the next few years, you should prepare by paying off those credit cards and only using them for emergencies. Do not cancel your existing cards since this may actually lower your credit score. By showing you have a low or zero balance on your credit cards, you will be showing lenders that you know how to use credit wisely and you have been paying your cards on time.

- Always pay bills on time

This includes your electric bill, rent, student loans, and other bills that you may have to pay each month. By creating a track record that can be traced, you will be showing lenders that you are a responsible person who deserves to have a home loan. It is a good idea to set your bank account up to pay the minimums on your accounts automatically. This way you are never late and never miss. Pay extra if you like but don't miss a payment.

What Makes Up My Credit Score

Credit scores and the formulas that the three major credit bureaus use are a closely guarded secret. However, in general, here are the five major areas that agencies look towards when determining your score.

- Payment History-35%

The most important component of your credit score looks at whether you can be trusted to repay money that is lent to you. This component considers the following factors:

- Have you paid your bills on time for each and every account on your credit report? Paying bills late has a negative effect on your score.

- If you've paid late, how late were you – 30 days, 60 days, or 90+ days? The later you are, the worse it is for your score.

- Have any of your accounts gone to collections? This is a red flag to potential lenders that you might not pay them back.

- Do you have any charge offs, debt settlements, bankruptcies, foreclosures, suits, wage attachments, liens or judgments against you? These are some of the worst things to have on your credit report from a lender's perspective.

- Amounts Owed-30%

The second-most important component of your credit score is how much you owe. It looks at the following factors:

o How much of your total available credit have you used? Less is better, but owning a little bit can be better than owing nothing at all because lenders want to see that if you borrow money, you are responsible and financially stable enough to pay it back.

o How much do you owe on specific types of accounts, such as a mortgage, auto loans, credit cards and installment amounts? Credit scoring software likes to see that you have a mix of different types of credit and that you manage them all responsibility.

o How much do you owe in total, and how much do you owe compared to the original amount on installment accounts? Again, less is better.

- Length of Credit History-15%

Your credit score also takes into account how long you have been using credit. How many years have you been using credit for? How old is your oldest account, and what is the average age of all your accounts? A long history is helpful (if it's not marred by late payments and other negative items), but a short history can be fine too as long as you've made your payments on time and don't owe too much.

- New Credit-10%

Your FICO score considers how many new accounts you have. It looks at how many new accounts you have applied for recently and when the last time you opened a new account was.

- Types of Credit in Use-10%

The final thing the FICO formula considers in determining your credit score is whether you have a mix of different types of credit, such as credit cards, store accounts, installment loans, and mortgages. It also looks at how many total accounts you have. Since this is a small component of your score, don't worry if you don't have accounts in each of these categories, and don't open new accounts just to increase your mix of credit types.

How Home Appraisals Can Affect Your Home Loan

Unfortunately, a home appraisal can affect the status of your loan. If the home appraisal comes under the selling price of the home, most lenders will not grant the loan as originally approved. They will typically lend a percentage of the appraised value and not the purchase price. This can be heartbreaking, but there are a few solutions that may work depending on the rules of the lender. The following options are available:

- ## The homeowner reduces the selling price

Depending on the appraised value in comparison to the asking price, some homeowners will be willing to lower the price of the home if they need to sell quickly.

You should not count on this happening since many homeowners want to receive the price they are asking for. You may have no choice but to find another home. In many cases however the appraised value will be the same with the next buyers so the seller will reduce as they understand this challenge will reoccur with every buyer

- ## A higher down payment

Some lenders will grant you the loan if you agree to pay a larger down payment on the home and assume the financial risk. This is only an option if you can afford to pay a larger down payment. Do not risk your financial security in these cases; it is just not worth it.

- ## Dispute the appraisal

You can dispute the appraised value. This is not based on your opinion or feeling of home worth. You must show that there are comparable home sales superior to those the appraiser used. Your real estate agent may help you with this. You can submit these to the lender and they can evaluate the validity of the appraisal.

- ## The mortgage timeline

Most mortgages can be closed in 30 days. In today's market, it is not uncommon to run into delays with lenders that might take up to 60 days to close your loan. Some lenders close loans in as little as 20 days, while another lender across the street might take as much as 60 days for the same loan transaction. This may also depend on your state, county and local laws and regulations.

· Find another lender

This is a last resort move because it will postpone the closing for another month or so, and there is no guarantee that the lender will have an appraisal with a different value. With some loans like FHA mortgages, the appraisal is attached to the property for months and going to another lender won't help as they will need to use the same appraisal report.

Since home appraisals are required by most lenders, you should find out during the loan application process the policies that the lender has when dealing with appraisals. If your lender will not accept a lower selling price, you putting down a larger down payment, or other solutions to a low appraisal, you should consider finding another lender just in case there are any problems down the road.

Home appraisals are based on the current value of homes in the neighborhood, homes that are comparable in size, the housing market, and the age of the home. While you can expect to hear different numbers from different appraisers, you will see that these numbers will usually not be too far off.

The only real benefit of a low home appraisal is that it will tell the homeowners to list the home for less money so that they will be able to sell it. In the meantime, you will have to find another home.

How Home Inspections Can Affect Your Home Loan

While a poor home inspection will usually not deter a lender from granting a home loan, you should be aware that some lenders will not grant a loan if there is termite damage or structural damage to the home due to water or age.

This will also lower the overall appraisal of the home, which could be another issue that lenders may have when deciding to approve a home loan.

If the home inspection is not favorable, ask your lender what will need to be done in order to rectify the problem. Many times removing the termites and correcting the water damage is all that will be needed. Many times homeowners will foot the bill for these types of repairs.

Additional Fees for Home Loans

You may notice that you have to pay small fees throughout your home buying experience. It seems that every piece of paper you sign, file, or request will cost you some money. Here is a list of fees that you may be charged:

- Credit report fee
- Loan discount fee
- Lender's inspection fee

- Appraisal fee
- Loan origination fee
- Mortgage insurance application fee
- Assumption fee
- Hazard insurance
- Title search, and
- Title insurance

These fees can add up, so you will want to be prepared and have a little extra in savings for when these fees come up. Some of these fees can be put off until the closing, but you should be planning for them in advance. Go over this with your lender to be fully informed in your situation.

Loan Estimates

When you make your official application, your lender is required by law to deliver a document called a Loan Estimate (LE for short). Although these are estimates, the lender cannot change many of the fees on the estimate so they are usually a good guide for costs and fees

When looking for a lender, you should compare estimates to see which lender is the lowest, which are the highest, and which are in the middle. All too often, these estimates are too low. Some lenders will do this on purpose in order to get you to take out the loan. By comparing estimates, you will be able to get a better idea of which lenders are honest and which are not.

As a rule, you should expect to pay between three and five percent of your loan in closing costs. The loan estimate will give you an idea of the final cost, but you should keep track of what everything costs and try to have extra money set aside just in case.

Prior to closing you will receive a Closing Disclosure (CD for short). It has a very similar format to the LE. This is so you can easily compare the two to ensure you understand any changes between the initial estimate and your final numbers

Escrow and Other Loans Terms

As you are going through the home loan process, you will run across a few terms that you will not understand. You should ask your lender to explain these terms so that you will fully understand the type of loan you are applying for, the lender policies, and other information that will be important throughout the life of the loan. Here are some common terms you may encounter:

- Escrow

While this term can mean different things in different situations, you will see it often when closing a home. If you place a down payment on a home, it will be in escrow until all the paperwork has been signed. The money is held by the seller's attorney in a special bank account "in escrow"

- Mortgage

Even though you have heard of a mortgage before, you probably thought of it as the home loan you will be paying once you move into your new home. Technically, a mortgage is a lien on your home created by the lender. If you cannot make payments on your home, the lender will have the right to sell the property in order to gain the money that they have lost.

- Foreclosure

This is a term that refers to homes whose owners could not make payments each month. Once a lender has decided to sell the home, it will be in foreclosure. You should find out ways to work with your lender in case you miss a mortgage payment at any time. Having this knowledge in advance will make financial emergencies easier to deal with.

- Mortgage Broker

A mortgage broker is a person who does not work for a bank, but rather works on commission to match homebuyers with many lenders that may not be in your area. In today's environment the minority of loans are done with a mortgage broker. They frequently have access to the exotic and non-standard loans but most people don't need that.

- Mortgage Banker

This refers to someone working with a direct lender who will originate mortgage loans. Frequently referred to as a loan officer or home mortgage consultant. This is the person who will be your primary interface and help you obtain your mortgage from the lender

- Points

This refers to prepaid interest on your loan. If you choose to pay points this may in turn lower your interest rate for the life of the loan and your payment. This is a way to pay a little more upfront to sometimes save big over the life of the loan. Discuss this with your Lender

- Down Payment

A down payment is helpful in several ways. It will lower the amount of money you will need for a home loan, it will allow lenders to see that you are responsible for paying off a mortgage, and it will move the home buying process faster. Most first time homeowners will put down no more than 20% for a down payment. There are many programs with 3% or 3.5% down payment and if you qualify for a VA loan (for veterans) you may qualify for 0% down

You do not want to overextend yourself by putting a huge down payment on a home because you may not have enough money to pay your mortgage, afford new furniture, or make home repairs.

- Debt to Income Ratio

This is one way that lenders will determine if you can afford your monthly mortgage payments on your current income. The lender will subtract all your recurring debt to determine how much is left for a mortgage payment.

This is why not buying a car or spending money on your credit cards is so important when buying a home. The less debt you have will mean more available money for your mortgage payment.

· Private Mortgage Insurance

When putting down less than 20% on your home purchase you will likely be subject to this insurance (PMI). This extra insurance will protect the lender in case you default on the loan by paying them at least 15% of the total loan value. This will cost you a little extra each month, but it may be required in order to obtain a loan.

Have a conversation with your lender about this as well as there are different kinds of PMI. Some people pay it all upfront as this may be cheaper in the long run. Some include it into the interest rate (frequently called Lender Paid PMI). This may be cheaper in the short term but more expensive in the long term. It depends on how long you intend to keep the home (or rather the mortgage). PMI on Conventional loans can be removed after a time. On some FHA loans PMI is there for the life of the loan. Have a conversation about your PMI if you are putting down less than 20% on your home purchase.

· Credit Report

Before you apply for a home loan, you should obtain copies of your credit report so that you can check for errors; see how much money you owe on credit cards and loans, and see what your credit score is. This is another way that lenders will determine if you will receive a loan.

The law provides that you can obtain a free copy of your credit report once per year from each of the three bureaus (EquiFax, TransUnion, Experian). GO to www.annualcreditreport.com for that report.

These are three credit reports that you should obtain, because you will not know which one the lender will scrutinize the most. Most lenders will review all three and review the information in all three. They typically the middle score for your credit score (not the average). While the numbers from these credit reports should not vary too much, if you see any major discrepancies caused by an error, you should contact the agency and have the mistake corrected. Beware! There are many companies selling credit reports or offering free one with this or that subscription or service. It is the FICO score most lenders use and not these other companies. To make things more confusing there are various FICO scores. The FICO score one gets when obtaining a credit card or automobile loan are not only different scoring models but they differ from the score used in mortgage finance. If you are looking at a service providing a credit score that is not FICO (read the fine print - is it "algorithmically similar") expect the score from the bank to be different. I've seen them one hundred points different. If the score your were provided is FICO, it still may be different if it is not the same scoring model used by the mortgage company. Don't be worried about this. Just know why the score may be different.

Chapter 7 - Making a Realistic Offer

By this point, you should have found a real estate agent, contacted your lender, and seen a few homes. If you have not made up your mind on a home yet, you should take your time and keep looking. But keep in mind that if you wait too long, you may end up in a bidding war with another buyer.

Making an offer on a home is a huge step. You will be taking on the responsibility of a mortgage, repairs, lawn care, and other chores that homeowners sometimes gripe too much about. While you should be cautious, you should also make a bid on a home that you really like within a week after seeing it. This will put your mind at ease so that you can think of all the other items you will have to get done before the closing.

What to do Before Making an Offer

Before you make an offer on a home, you should do the following:

- Attend open houses

Attend as many open houses as you can in homes that are in the area where you want to live. This will give you the opportunity to see what is out there, the going price of homes in the area, and also give you a basis of comparison when looking at other homes.

- Find out more about a property

If you find a home that you might want to buy, you should find out everything you can about the property first before making an offer. Visit the county clerk's office or go online to learn more about the property. This will give you an idea of how much you should offer for the home. If the home is in an area that has seen better days, then you can make an offer that is less because when you sell the property someday, you may have to lower your price as well.

- Find out more about taxes in the area

As a homeowner, you will be paying yearly property taxes, local taxes, school taxes, community dues, and other taxes that could drive your household spending through the roof. Before you commit to living in a certain area, make sure you understand everything you will be paying each year.

Your real estate agent should have the neighborhood information that will help you decide where you want to move. You can also visit your local tax office and see how much the current homeowners paid in taxes last year.

When you visit a lender, you will have to figure in your taxes as household expenses. This will be deducted from your income, which will leave you with less each month to pay your mortgage.

Just because you have found a home that is within your budget, you may not be able to afford the taxes that come with it.

These suggestions will help you make the most informed decision possible when it comes to buying your first home.

How to Write a Purchase Offer

This is the most important step when making an offer to buy your first home. In some places the homebuyer does this and in others a professional does this for the home buyer. In some places the written offer is simple or a form and in other places it can be quite lengthy and detailed. The purchase offer should outline everything you expect from the homeowner and what they can expect from you. You should include the following in your offer:

- Price being offered
- Amount of deposit on the home
- Amount of money you will be putting down on the home
- Contingencies (such as appliances that will stay, repairs that will need to be made, removal of items in the yard, etc.)
- When closing will take place
- Specify who will pay which fees, and
- Any reports that will be needed

Each of these categories should be explained in its own paragraph. Many states have their own laws concerning contingency, the amount of time a buyer has to respond to the offer, and fees that are to be paid. Your real estate agent is aware of these laws and will put your offer together and present it for you.

Discuss more than just the price you are offering with your real estate agent. They may have some advice or additional categories you should add depending on the age of the home, the neighborhood, and the laws that exist. The down payment amount or other terms may become important. If you make an offer that is reasonable, well written, and hard to break, then you will be on your way to buying a home.

Making an Offer

After completing your research, you will be ready to make an offer on your first home. You will have to visit your real estate agent to sign a formal agreement that will outline your offer and for how long you will be making this offer. Most agreements will give sellers three days to a week to consider the offer.

In this time, the offer may be accepted, rejected, or a counter offer will be made. You will have to decide what you will want to do next if the offer is rejected or another offer is made. If the offer is accepted, then you will have to contact your lender, home inspector, and make arrangements for your move.

Low or High Offers

Hopefully, by researching the neighborhood, the property, and the value of the home, you will be able to come as close to the seller's price as possible. Sometimes, though, this is not possible.

There may be circumstances that may prohibit you from making an offer that is close to the selling price.

Low Offers

Low offers are usually the result of the selling price being too high, ignorance of the buyer, or the buyer not having enough money to pay the asking price. Whatever the reasons, you should be careful when giving a low offer to a homeowner.

If you have specific reasons for offering a lower price, they should be mentioned in the offer so that the homeowner has a better understanding of how you came to the price offered. In some cases, the seller may offer a counteroffer, which you can either accept or reject. But, if the homeowner feels insulted by the lower offer, they may just reject the offer and move on to another.

High Offers

The only time you should make an offer that is higher than the asking price is if other offers have been made. While this could be the beginning of a bidding war, if you offer just a little more than the highest bid, you may win. You should only do this if the property is worth it and you will be living in it for a long time.

If you make an offer that is high, then you will not leave any room for negotiation. Depending on the homeowner's circumstances, they may have been willing to go a little lower in order to sell the home. But since you made an offer that was higher than the asking price, you will end up paying more than you should have.

Many times, first time home buyers make the mistake of wanting a home so badly that they are willing to pay a few thousand more than the home is worth. This is money that could be used for a down payment.

Making the Right Offer

The closer you can come to the asking price, the better off you will be. Once the home inspection is complete, the homeowners may have to come down in price anyway because of the repairs that will have to be made.

Making the right decisions when buying a home are not always made quickly. You should play by the rules and just see what happens. If you get into a bidding war and cannot bid any higher, then it is best to let the home go and find another. You should not be a slave to your first home by buying one that is over your budget. There are many homes that are available if you keep looking.

How to Handle a Counter Offer and Offer Rejection

Sometimes, if you give homeowners an offer that is lower than their asking price, they may offer you a counter offer. This is usually an offer that is more than your offer, but a little less than the asking price.

Discrimination

We don't want to but yes we must discuss this again. The Fair Housing Act of 1968 covers housing discrimination as mentioned earlier. This law prohibits housing discrimination by real estate firms and homeowners. This means that homeowners may not refuse to lease or sell property based on race, religion, gender, color, or national origin.

Anyone found in violation of this law can face financial penalties. A homeowner can discriminate based on poor credit or loan terms.

You may suspect illegal discrimination if
- Someone tells you a listed home is no longer for sale but it remains on the market
- An agent avoids showing you homes in areas you have requested without a sufficient explanation
- A seller refuses a full-priced offer

If you believe you are being illegally discriminated against you can request a complaint form by calling the federal Department of Housing and Urban Development (HUD) at 1-800-424-8590. They are tasked with investigating such complaints.

Counter Offer

Typically, the number of counter offers is limitless, but no counter offer can be the same. While counter offers are usually concerning money, these offers may also contain the following:

- o Ownership of appliances
- o Repairs
- o Time frames for closing, and
- o Time frames for counter offers
- o Seller's Concessions(a way to roll the closing costs into the mortgage)

Buyers and sellers may only have hours to accept, reject, or offer another counter offer after receiving one. This can be a very stressful process, especially if you are dealing with a seller that has other offers on the table. While most homeowners will reject an offer if it is too low or they have received another, some will try to get the most they can from the sale that can include the smallest items in the home.

If you are determined to buy a home, but still want a lower price after the buyer has reacted with a counter offer, you can try to find a price that will suit everyone's needs. If you are making a counter offer that does not make that much difference, you should weigh the odds that another offer has been made, the homeowner will reject your offer, and that time is ticking for everyone.

Try your best to accept the counteroffer before making one of your own. Is it really worth losing your dream home over one or two thousand dollars?

Dealing with Rejection

The hardest part about an offer rejection is that the homeowner does not have to answer your offer. If you do not hear from the homeowner within a week, it is safe to assume they are not interested in your bid. While this can be frustrating, you will have to move on. Begin your house hunting again and try to stay positive.

If the homeowner gives you a response in the form of a rejection, they may site the reason why in the paperwork. If your offer was too low, they had another offer, decided not to sell, or want to wait for a higher offer, at least you can move on without wondering why our bid was rejected.

Considering Items in the Home

When you are writing your purchase offer, you should consider the items that you would like to keep and the items you would like to have removed from the home. These items can include:

- Certain appliances (such as washer and dryer)
- Lighting fixtures
- Storage fixtures
- Single air conditioning units that fit into windows
- Hardware from windows and doors, or
- Pools

You should put these items in writing so that you will get them with the home. Some homeowners may try taking certain items with them either because they didn't know that you wanted them or because they were not supposed to be sold with the home to begin with. Be sure to obtain a list of items the homeowner is selling with the home so that you can compare it to your list.

This can also work in reverse. If there are items that you would like removed from the home or property before you move in, you should specify these in the offer. These items can include:

- Old patio furniture
- Mechanical equipment
- Old appliances, and
- Light fixtures

By putting all of these items in writing, you will be helping to move the buying process along. While the homeowners may not agree with everything that you may want to keep, it will be up to them if they want to continue the process. Having everything in writing will leave people with no surprises during the closing.

Understanding the Seller

One of the key elements of making a solid offer is having an understanding of the seller. Your real estate agent will be able to tell you a little bit about the seller that may help when trying to come up with a fair offer.

When deciding on an offer for a home, you should find out the following about the seller:

- How eager are they to sell their home?
- How long have they lived in the home?

- How many offers have they received?
- How many have they turned down?
- Have they lowered their asking price?
- Are they relocating to another area?
- Do they need to sell their home quickly?
- Are they waiting for their asking price?

What to do in a Buyer's Market

In a buyer's market, you will have more choices when it comes to the types of homes you can purchase.

Depending on how long the market favors the buyer, you will also have the luxury of taking your time because bidding wars are much less. When buying your first home, you should check out all your options. That home you couldn't afford a few years ago may be in your price range today.

When looking for a home in a buyer's market, you should do the following:

- Stay current with listings in your area
- Sign up for free email listings and newsletters
- Check out homes that have recently been reduced
- When making an offer, consider a seller's concession
- See if there are other offers, such as appliances that come with the home
- Ask for certain allowances (carpeting, roofing, siding, etc.)
- Do not be afraid to offer a lower price, and
- Ask for a shorter response time

In a buyer's market, homeowners may offer these options to you as an incentive to buy their homes. They may also offer warranties on appliances that you should take advantage of.

There are dangers that you should consider when buying in a buyer's market, however.

- If you are not planning on living in the home for more than three years, you may want to wait until the market changes or plan to live in the home longer. Many times, market trends can last for a few years. If you need to move after a year or so, you may have difficulty finding a buyer and you may have to sell the home for less than what you paid for it.
- While most homeowners stay in their homes for at least two years in order to save money in taxes, marketing trends have been known to last longer. You should be prepared for this when buying your first home.
- Make sure a thorough home inspection has been completed before buying the home. If you decide you cannot live there after you have bought the property, you may have difficulty selling it, and you will have to spend more money making repairs.

Even though you cannot predict how the market will change, you should consider a home that you can afford, that you will want to live in for a long time, and one that can be improved upon while you own it.

What to do in a Seller's Market

In a seller's market, you will have to play the game slightly different than you would in a buyer's market. In this type of market, there are many buyers who will want to buy homes that are attractive and priced within their budget. Homeowners will have their pick of offers to choose from so your offer will have to stand out in more than just price.

When looking for a home in a seller's market, you should:

- Make an offer that is close to the asking price or slightly over
- Send a pre-qualification or better yet a preapproval letter from your lender with the offer (best is a fully underwritten pre approval - ask your lender for this if they offer it)
- Choose a closing date that is sooner rather than later
- Do not ask for too many contingencies
- Promise more of a down payment, and
- Use a real estate agent that gets things done quickly

In a seller's market, you may also want to think about the dangers of buying a home. If you make an offer that is too high and you find out later on that the mortgage payments will be a struggle. Be sure to discuss payments with your lender so you are clear what you are getting in to. Remember that sometimes you can be approved for a payment that lender says is ok but it is more than you want to handle.

Buying your first home during this time may also be difficult because you will not be able to put much down, you may only qualify for a certain amount of money which may not be enough to compete during a bidding war, and you may be outbid by those who have more experience than you do.

When you decide to buy a home, you should be looking at your financial situation, the market, and the asking price for the homes you are interested in making an offer on. If you can wait a few months to see where the market is headed, then maybe this is the best way to save more money and find a home that is affordable. This is a waiting game that no one wants to play, but may be necessary, especially if this is your first home purchase.

Seller's markets and buyer's markets have their advantages and disadvantages, but in the end, the offer that you make will determine whether your offer will be accepted.

Chapter 8 - Contracts, Home Warranties and the Closing

Drawing up contracts, having the final walkthrough, and going to the closing are the last steps you will have to take when buying your first home. This is the time when having a real estate agent you can trust, and a little knowledge of home buying comes in handy.

But, what about all of those other miscellaneous fees that will come up before and during the closing? You should be aware of additional fees when you apply for a loan and when you are closing on your new home.

Contracts

Your purchase offer, once accepted leads to a purchase contract in most places. It is not required by law that you work with an attorney in most states. In some areas it is common and customary and in some areas it is not. In my years of experience I suggest you go with common and customary for you areas. I have seen a couple of people go forward without an attorney in places that expect one and not only did it not work out, it cost money for those attempting it. I have seen people in areas that do not use attorneys, hire one and pay for something that was not necessary.

Typically the seller's side draws up the contract (it may be the realtor or the attorney depending on where you are buying) and sends it to your realtor or attorney. Your attorney will mark it up or make changes discussed with you and the seller's attorney. Once everyone is in agreement, your attorney will have you sign the contract and send it back to the seller along with an agreed upon down payment or part of the down payment. The seller's attorney will review the changes and have their client (the seller) countersign. This is called a fully executed contract. The fully executed version will be sent to your attorney and now you are officially "in contract". You will want your attorney to send a copy of that fully executed contract to your lender so they may begin processing your mortgage loan. This process could be a little different if you live somewhere or are buying somewhere without the attorney involvement.

Contingencies

Real estate contingencies can be added onto an existing contract or can be created as a separate contract depending on what you would like to include in the purchase offer. Contingencies can include a wide range of items, including:

- Home inspections and pest inspections
- Home appraisals
- Financing
- Septic system tests
- Appliances that will stay in the home, and
- Mortgage

You will need to include a resolution for repairs that may need to be done before you can move into the home. If it is agreed upon in writing that the homeowners will take care of all or some repairs that may be found during a home inspection, this will save time later on.

Your attorney will also include ways to get out of the deal that include loan denial, repairs that cannot be fixed, and lead, mold, or radon that is found in the home. Having a way out of the contract will save you money and time.

If you are buying a home that is for sale by owner (FSBO), that is all the more reason to work with an attorney that is willing to help you create a contingency list and edit it where necessary. Do not rely on the seller's agent because they are after their client's best interests and not necessarily yours. If you are working with a buyer's agent, that person is working on your behalf and not the seller.

Builder Contracts

If you are buying a new home from a builder, you will have to sign a builder's contract that states you have the financial means to pay for a new home, that you have decided on a location for your new home, and that you are ready to build.

You should hire an attorney at this point to go over the contract to see if there are any problems that will have to be ironed out before you begin building the home.

Disclosures

Once you send your fully executed contracts to your lender, they will send you various disclosures to begin your official approval process and loan commitment. Your contract will likely have a date by which you must have this loan commitment. That shows you are officially approved and your lender has committed to making the loan. There are normally some conditions attached to that initial commitment such as you still being employed at the time of closing, the home having a value to justify the loan, you having the money to close, etc.

These disclosures are not binding. They will include estimates and general numbers. Signing them simply acknowledges you are applying for a loan. It does not lock an interest rate or oblige you to anything.

Home Warranties

If you are buying an older home, you may want to purchase a home warranty that will cover repairs that will have to be made during your first year of ownership. There are various companies that specialize in the product. You can find them online or your real estate agent may have a recommendation. I have even seen some agents use the warranty as a marketing tool to help sell a home.

While a home inspection will catch any immediate repairs, no one can foresee an oven falling apart or a dryer burning out. Since you may not have a lot of extra money left over after paying for closing costs, down payment, and mortgage payments, having extra insurance will allow you to make the repairs you will need.

Most policies will cost a few hundred dollars. Coverage will begin the day of your closing and will last for a year. You will have the option of renewing the policy if you would like at that time. If you need to have an appliance repaired, you may have to pay a small co-pay at the time of the repair.

Not all policies are the same, so you should do your research to find the best deal. Compare the types of repairs that are covered under the policies and choose the one that fits your home.

Final Walkthrough

The final walkthrough of the home will take place before the closing. This is the final chance for you to see the home before it becomes yours. This was discussed in detail earlier in the book. Make sure the items on your contingency are in place so that you can sign the contracts

Closing

When you finally arrive at the closing, you should expect to:

- Sign documents
- Deliver the remainder of any down payment not already paid
- Pay closing costs, and
- Get your keys

The closing can take an hour or two, but usually moves quickly because there is little left to do. At the closing you will probably meet the homeowners. This could be the first time you will meet them. This is a good time to ask if there is anything about the home you will need to know.

Signing

There is a lot to sign at the closing. There will be a pile of documents from your lender and more documents which convey ownership of the property. In some cases there are other documents due to special circumstances. Many of these documents will require you to sign more than one copy so you may be signing lots of times. Fortunately technology is touching this part of the process too. More and more states are allowing many documents to be signed electronically. More and more lenders are adopting this and making the closing shorter duration and less stressful.

Paying Closing Costs and Down Payment

Typically, the buyer will have to pay the closing costs associated with buying a home. In some cases some or all of your closing costs may have been rolled into your loan. This is normally done with a seller's concession and you would be well aware of this ahead of time. Otherwise you are responsible for paying most of the closing costs. The seller may have to pay some as well.

You will also pay any remaining down payment. For example if you were putting 20% down, your attorney may have advised and negotiated putting 10% at contract and the balance at closing. In this example you will be responsible for bringing those funds to the closing. Your attorney will advise and instruct how to do this. If you didn't have an attorney in this transaction, you will bring whatever additional funds were specified in the contract and in the way the contract specified them.

Get Your Keys

After signing at the closing, you will receive the keys to your new home. This is an exciting feeling and one that will be with you for a long time. Take a picture. Make this a big deal. When I closed on my first home I didn't understand how that one act would cascade and multiply and have suce a beneficial impact on not only my net worth but for those who come after me. I am accumulating net worth that my sons will use to get their start. This is what my parents did for me. This is what I do for my offspring. My father always says that so many people leave nothing for their children but a name. Some leave debt for their children. Don't let that be you. These keys represent something bigger.

Conclusion

When it comes to purchasing a home you will find that it takes time. Be patient. You will have several homes shown to you before you make the decision to buy. There are some real estate agents who will show you many in a day. How many homes that you see are completely up to you and how good your real estate agent is.

The real estate agent will ask you some basic questions about price and features, but a good real estate agent will find you a house within a few shows. Why? Because everyone knows that a good real estate agent will be able to match a home with the couple's personality. When you go with your real estate agent to purchase a home you should get plenty of rest the day before and you need to eat a hearty meal because you don't want to quit early in the day because you don't feel well.

At last, you will want to make sure that everything goes according to plan so that you can have a smooth adjustment into owning a home.

This page intentionally left blank [well now that we put this here, it is not really blank is it?]

Made in USA - North Chelmsford, MA
1171817_9798625160674
02.09.2022 0949